COWBOY
COLLECTIBLES

Syroco pressed-wood western-style bookends, c. 1934.

COWBOY COLLECTIBLES

by Robert Heide and John Gilman

Timothy Bissell, Chief Photographer

(with additional photography by Priscilla Cammarano)

1817

HARPER & ROW, PUBLISHERS, New York

Cambridge, Philadelphia, San Francisco, London
Mexico City, São Paulo, Sydney

By the same authors:

Dime-Store Dream Parade: Popular Culture 1925–1955

All uninitialed photographs were taken by chief photographer Timothy Bissell. Theodore Hake provided some photographs of his collectibles, and these are marked (T.H.). Other collectibles from Mr. Hake's collection were photographed on a field trip by Mr. Bissell. Photographs by Priscilla Cammarano are marked (P.C.).

Those items not attributed to others ("collection of" or "courtesy of") are from the cowboy collection of the co-authors, John Gilman and Robert Heide.

"Roy Rogers," p. xiv: Words and music Bernie Taupin, music Elton John. Copyright © 1973 Dick James Music Ltd., 5 Theobalds Road, London, England WC1X8SE. All rights to the United States and Canada controlled by Dick James Inc., 24 Music Square East, Nashville, Tennessee 37212. All rights reserved.

"Texas Cattle Ranching," pp. 3–4: From *The Cattlemen,* copyright © 1958 by Mari Sandoz, used by permission of Hastings House, Publishers, New York.

Tom Mix Ralston commercial, p. 50: Used with the permission of the Ralston Purina Company.

"Back in the Saddle Again," p. 92: Used by permission of Western Music Publishing Company.

"Take Me Back to My Boots and Saddle," p. 92: Used by permission of Largo Music Inc., administrator of Whitcup Music Inc., Criscott Music Co.

Howdy Doody song, "Never-ever-ever pick a fight," p. 160: Permission granted by Bob Smith.

FIRST EDITION

Designer: Sheila Lynch

Library of Congress Cataloging in Publication Data

Heide, Robert, date
   Cowboy collectibles.
   (Harper colophon books)
   Includes index.
   1. Cowboys—Collectibles—United States. I. Gilman,
John, date.   II. Title.
NK823.H4 1982   978   82–47552
ISBN 0–06–090985–4 (pbk.)   AACR2

82 83 84 85 86 10 9 8 7 6 5 4 3 2 1

ACKNOWLEDGMENTS

Thanks to the following organizations for their help with this project: The Red Pony Rodeo in Lakewood, New Jersey; Stetson's "World's Toughest Rodeo" at Madison Square Garden; Dr. Reba Collins, Curator, Will Rogers Memorial, Claremore, Oklahoma; Buffalo Bill Memorial Museum, Denver Department of Parks & Recreation in Golden, Colorado; The Daughters of the Republic of Texas in San Antonio; Willie Nelson; Kinky Friedman; The Lone Star Café in New York; National Cowboy Hall of Fame and Western Heroes, Oklahoma City, Oklahoma; Amon Carter Museum in Fort Worth; Roy Rogers Museum, Victorville, California; University of Texas, Institute of Texan Culture, San Antonio; University of Texas, Humanities Research Center, Austin; University of Wyoming, American Heritage Center in Laramie; Smithsonian Institution, National Museum of Natural History, National Anthropological Archives, Washington, D.C.; City of Dallas; Arizona Photographic Association in Phoenix; Country Music Foundation in Nashville, Tennessee; the Oregon Historical Society in Portland; University of Oklahoma in Norman.

We also appreciate the contributions made by the following New York stores: Chisholm Gallery, Phases, Fiorucci, Serendipity, Second Hand Rose, Richard

Western Big Little Book Collection. Top: The Lone Ranger and the Red Renegades *(1939);* Bobby Benson on the H-Bar-O Ranch *(1934);* Chester Gump at Silver Creek Ranch *(1934);* Tom Mix and the Hoard of Montezuma *(1937).* *Bottom:* Red Ryder the Fighting Westerner *(1940);* Billy the Kid *(1935); Zane Grey's* Tex Thorne Comes out of the West *(1937);* Chief Wahoo and the Lost Pioneers *(1942);* Dixie Dugan Among the Cowboys *(1939);* Buffalo Bill Plays a Lone Hand *(1936). (P.C.)*

Utilla, Topeo, Depression Modern, Classic Collectibles, Peanut Butter and Jane, A Touch of Us, Mythology, Cinemabilia, Stewart and Judy of Reminiscence, and Johnny Jupiter.

Thanks to all these folks who helped and have been supportive: David Sterling, Huck Snyder, Tom Ellis, Ron Link, Leah D. Frank, Manuel Garza, Betty Brown, Karl Laub, Dwight Goss, George Shail, Drew Van Husen, Peter and Evelyn Cammarano, Linda Eskenas, Robert Patrick, Billy Hoffman, Edward Albee, Andy Warhol, Sandy Turner, Marguerite Young, Jim Boyle, John Moses, Robert Dahdah, John Carney, Peter Gilman, Elliot Sherman, Belman Promotions, Albert Poland, Marie-Louise Odstrcil, Henry Mazzeo, Fred Orlansky, Norma Edgar, Frances McComish Woodruff, Jack J. Wells, Rochelle Oliver, Ken Ketwig, Tim Bissell, Jim Hans—Hoboken Historian, Paul Aaron of "Cowboy Joe's Radio Ranch" on WKCR-FM, Adele and George Spear of Mother Hubbard's Restaurant in Elizabeth, New Jersey, Angelina of Pennyfeathers, Tom Snyder, and John Margolies.

Special acknowledgments to: Robert Lesser, author of *A Celebration of Comic Art and Memorabilia;* Kenneth Anger, filmmaker extraordinaire and author of *Hollywood Babylon;* Joe Franklin of WOR-TV; Don Berman, production, NBC-TV; Howard Smith and Lin Harris of the *Village Voice;* Vicki Gold Levi, author of *Atlantic City: 125 Years of Ocean Madness;* Bill and Barbara Baranyay of the New Jersey Audubon Society; Lawrence P. Ashmead and Craig D. Nelson of Harper & Row; and Lois de la Haba for their contributions to this book. Special thanks also to a real cowboy pal, Theodore L. Hake, who led us into a secret mystery silver mine of cowboy collectibles. To receive Ted Hake's Auction Catalogue specializing in pop-culture Western memorabilia and other nostalgia collectibles, please write to: Hake's Americana Collectibles, P.O. Box 1444, York, Pennsylvania 17405, or call 717-843-3731.

Ted Hake in his Hopalong Cassidy outfit, 1950s.

This book is dedicated to the memory of Joe Cino,
whose Rough-Rider cowboy spirit
and pioneering Caffè Cino Theatre
began the off-off Broadway movement
that changed theatrical history for all time.

CONTENTS

PREFACE:
A COWBOY DREAM

The cowboy is a true national hero of American culture. In *Cowboy Collectibles* we'll be looking at the twentieth-century descendants of the original—latter-day cowboys like Tom Mix, Roy Rogers, Gene Autry and Hopalong Cassidy—and at the commercial items and tie-in products associated with them, many of which are now hard-to-find collector's items.

First, though, we'll examine those origins—the world of the actual nineteenth-century American cowboy who spent his hard-working days on the ranches and open ranges of the Wild West. These men created and embodied the idea of "cowboy" as we think of it today and were the predecessors of the popular-culture cowboy folk heroes who later emerged out of the decline of the Old West. The old-style cowboys—driving large herds of cattle up the early trails, holding six-gun shoot-outs in lawless freewheeling cow towns like Abilene and Dodge City, singing lonesome songs while drinking coffee over an open campfire—existed in the pure sense for just about twenty years. This period of the cowboy lasted from the end of the Civil War until the 1880s, when it was halted by the proliferation of the railroads, the homesteader ranches with their new barbed-wire fences that cut across the old trails (cutting the noses of cows and wild horses as well), and the entrance of eastern big business concerns into the cattle-ranching field, boardroom speculators who brought the beef industry to Wall Street.

This cowboy history—the story of rough-hewn individualists who confronted the el-

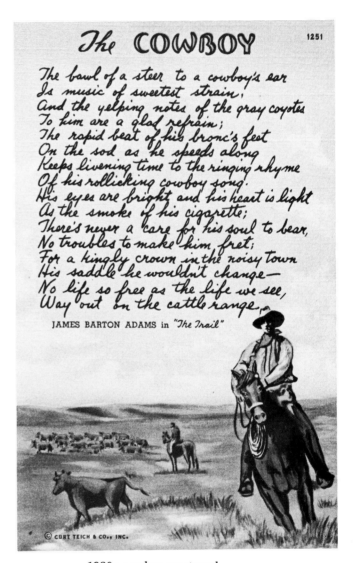

1930s cowboy postcard.

ements of the vast western plains—served as the basis for the later mythologizing of the Wild West in tent shows, circuses, rodeos, silent and talking pictures, radio and television shows, and country and western music. This melodramatic call to the West just as it began to decline also attracted a slew of writers who romanticized the cowboy's life for an American public ever hungry for some of the excitement and adventure of the western frontier.

A cowboy today is accepted by his peers only if he can perform certain skills such as bronco-busting, steer wrestling, and bull roping, and if he has also worked a ranch

Pendleton Round-up

PENDLETON, OREGON

© PENDLETON ROUND-UP

WALLACE SMITH
PENDLETON

LET'ER BUCK

OFFICIAL SOUVENIR PROGRAM

or has done a stint on the rodeo circuit. The sport of rodeo is as demanding and dangerous as any, pitting man against beast just as in the days of the early Roman gladiators. Dan Dailey, one of the top rodeo cowboys of today, has said, "Rodeo is the toughest sport of all. Them bulls weigh anywhere from 1800 to 2200 pounds and you have to ride them for eight seconds. Most cowboys only weigh 150 to 175 pounds. In all other sports, competitors are matched up against people of the same weight." Today's cowboys may be a modern version of the old, but they often seem misplaced and lost in our technological age as they stomp on cement sidewalks or hang out in a shopping-center game room. What's more, the romantic western landscape now requires governmental environmental protection lest it disappear altogether.

The cowboy collectibles pictured in this book are the stuff of the golden age of cowboy pop culture: radio and early TV giveaways and commercial tie-in products, most of which were originally sent through the mail in exchange for a Ralston pouring-spout seal (and a dime), or two Ralston box-top labels, or sold in dime stores and department stores from the 1920s through the 1950s. Many of these items were mass-produced to fulfill the fantasies of American children and adults who dreamed of their own home on the range—even with the danger of invading Indians and outlaw villains—during the Depression, World War II, and on into the 1950s, when boys and girls peered into a little rectangular home screen at Roy, Gene, or Hoppy. Today these cowboy legends are alive and well. Perhaps the dream of the cowboy might be described as an escape into a better, simpler, less complex era; but there is little doubt that America is back in the saddle—ridin' the range—once more.

Cowboy collectibles are not bona fide antiques of the Old West such as Wenzel Friedrich horn tables, early cypress-wood cabinets, wagon wheels, enamel cooking ware, guns, saddles, barbed wire, pot-belly stoves, early railroadiana, or the covered wagons themselves. These antiques—now extremely high in price—have been documented thoroughly in other books and are collected by major museums. Painters of the frontier such as Alfred Jacob Miller, George Catlin, Karl Bodmer, Albert Bierstadt, Charles M. Russell and Frederic Remington, classic artists of the Old West, have also been extensively studied, and today their works sell in the six-figure range. Remington's bronze sculptures of cowboys and horses are highly sought after, although almost 60 percent are said to be reproductions and are often difficult even for experts to authenticate.

What we are concerned with here is the "new" antiques in this western idiom, sometimes referred to as nostalgia antiques, as memorabilia, or as just collectibles. Many of the cowboy collectibles in this book are sought after with a fervor almost as intense as that for cattle or gold once was, but many also are still to be found in flea markets, antique shops and shows, garage sales, and auctions, although prices are constantly on the rise as the popularity of things western increases. This is one reason we have decided not to provide a price guide, but we will say that any of these collectibles would represent a worthwhile investment today. A Tom Mix mystery ring or Roy Rogers cap gun found by a collector in an antique market can bring alive once again those memories of cowboy radio shows, movies, and early TV western adventures. Reading a dime novel or a Big Little Book or seeing a cowboy coloring book can also bring back to life the super-cowboys and their deeds of heroism. Included also in our study are certain cow-

Pendleton Round-up Official Souvenir Program, September 23, 1933. Collection of Oregon Historical Society, Portland.

Roy Rogers postcard, c. 1940s.

boy fashions from the recent past as well as western-style decorative items such as curtains, wallpaper, drinking tumblers, rugs, and bedspreads that might have been seen in the den, kitchen, bathroom, or boys' room back in the days of the golden age of cowboy culture. Tom Mix, Gene Autry, Roy Rogers, Hopalong Cassidy—and some of the "real" cowboys who became "reel" cowboys when the buffalo roamed no more, the Indian was on the dole, and the legends of the West came alive only through radio fantasy and movie dreams—are examined in this book as to their impact on popular culture.

A lyric sung by rock singer Elton John in his album *Goodbye Yellow Brick Road* is dedicated to and entitled "Roy Rogers," but it could just as easily have been written for Tom, Gene, or Hoppy.

> Sometimes you dream
> sometimes it seems
> there's nothing there at all.
> You just seem older than yesterday,
> And you're waiting for tomorrow to call.
> You draw to the curtains
> and one thing's for certain
> you're cozy in your little room.
> The carpet's all paid for,
> God bless the T.V.
> Let's go shoot a hole in the moon.
>
> And Roy Rogers is riding tonight
> Returning to our silver screens.
> Comic book characters never grow old,
> Evergreen heroes whose stories were told.
> The great sequin cowboy
> who sings of the plains
> of roundups and rustlers
> and home on the range.
> Turn on the T.V.
> shut out the lights—
> Roy Rogers is riding tonight.

And so another installment of the cowboy dream of western adventure begins.

COWBOY
COLLECTIBLES

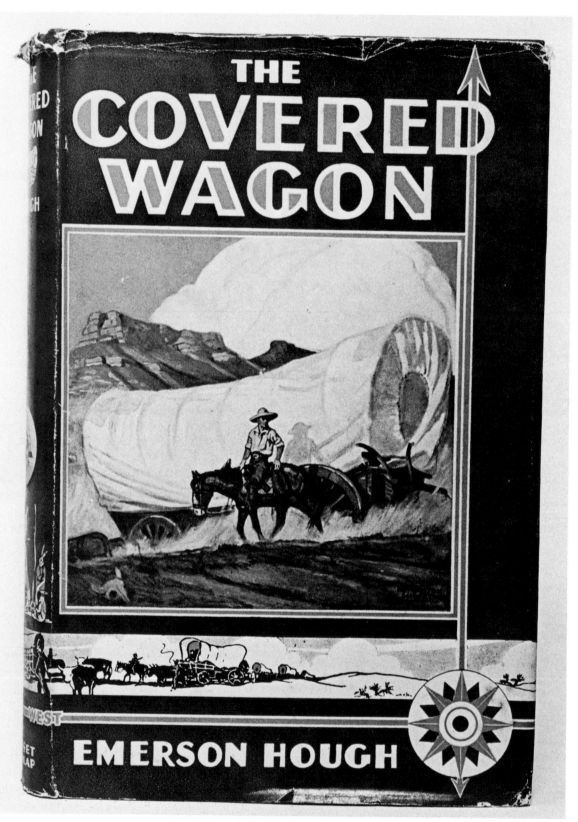

The Covered Wagon, *a novel of the pioneer days, by Emerson Hough, with original dust jacket, Grosset & Dunlap, 1922.*

COWBOY COUNTRY

VAQUEROS

When Christopher Columbus set sail for the second time to the New World, he brought with him about twenty-five stallions, ten mares, and a small herd of cattle. These animals were the first of this kind of domesticated livestock to arrive in the western hemisphere. They were unloaded in Haiti on January 2, 1494, and represented the beginnings of vast changes to come on the newly discovered continent.

In 1519, Hernando Cortés brought the first horses (eleven stallions and five mares) to New Spain (Mexico). Following this, just six months before Cortés defeated the Aztecs and captured what is now Mexico City, Gregorio de Villalobos arrived in New Spain, bringing with him the first cattle to this region.

By the 1560s government officials, miners, and men of the church had become the new rancher aristocracy in Mexico. As there was little other than land and livestock to invest in, ranches were soon owned by men from Mexico City, Puebla, and Querétaro. They hired Spanish *estancieros,*

overseers, for their ranches. Working for either a fixed wage or a small share of the profits, the estancieros employed a labor force of vaqueros (cowboys), many of whom were mestizos (mixed Spanish and Indian ancestry) or mulattos (mixed black and white ancestry). Some slaves brought from Africa through Spain were set free in the New World and became vaqueros. A vaquero spent sunrise to sunset at work on the plains; his only worldly possessions were his horse, his saddle, a short lance, and the clothing he wore.

By the mid-1500s there were vast herds of cattle and horses running free in New Spain, their increase aided by the Spanish custom of leaving stallions and bulls uncastrated. At first Indians feared the horses, these "big dogs" brought into their territory; but soon they began to capture and ride them.

Just as in the Old World, in New Spain cattle were equated with capital, a man's wealth, and they were rounded up regularly by vaqueros. This activity became known as the rodeo—from the Spanish word *rodear,* which means "to surround."

1

Rodeo later would be referred to in the American West as "roundup." The job of the vaquero was to drive the cattle from all directions toward a particular area where they could be sorted out. Calves would be branded and the cattle slaughtered for beef.

During the middle to late 1500s, certain "bad-blooded," lawless vaqueros banded together to ramble across the country stealing whatever they wanted. These *banditos* were the forerunners of the nineteenth-century outlaws of the American West like the James brothers or the Dalton gang. Feared by honest cowboys as violent cutthroats, they were nevertheless hired by ranchers, who would rather have them working for them than against them; so it happened that many vaqueros moving herds of cattle to market or for grazing were of the criminal-outlaw temperament.

By the end of the sixteenth century, cattle ranching with its vaqueros had moved steadily northward into what is now Texas and southern California, and thus the roots of the American cowboy were established.

COWBOY COUNTRY

California

By 1769, cattle, horses, and mules in large numbers were being moved into southern California by ship and by land. The Spanish found the California land perfect for grazing and were quick to establish the mission ranches of San Antonio, San Gabriel, and San Luis Obispo. Forts were constructed by Spanish soldiers at San Diego, Monterey, and other locations considered strategic. The mission was one of the earli-

Vegetable crate label depicting a galloping, roping vaquero on the western plains, c. 1945. Courtesy Chisholm Gallery, New York.

est centers of civilization in California; they obtained use but not title to public land for farming and grazing purposes. At the height of their power, there were twenty-one missions in California with ever-increasing herds of cattle. When Mexico achieved independence from Spain in 1821, influential Californians demanded that the new government in Mexico City restore to public domain the land held by the missions. By 1835 the lands were distributed by the Mexican government and passed into the hands of private ranchers. Angry vaqueros (working for the priests) slaughtered over half a million mission cattle before the new land was taken over.

The California valley, like the Texas prairie, was a magnet that attracted American pioneers from the eastern settlements. The Mexican influence over California weakened, making inevitable California's revolt for independence in 1846.

Texas: The Beginnings

During the period when Mexico was achieving its independence, the Texas missions, numbering about fifty, were also being abandoned, the priests sometimes slaughtering or releasing their cattle or handing them over to Indians.

Moses Austin, an early Texas settler, was given a land grant by Mexico of 200,000 acres along the Colorado River. In 1821, at his son Stephen's invitation (Moses died on the return trip from San Antonio), 297 colonists came to Texas from Louisiana, Arkansas, and Alabama. Later these people were called The Old Three Hundred by Texans. Farmers received 177 acres each, while those raising cattle were given 4,428 acres at 12½ cents an acre. The Texas land was rich, the livestock thrived, and the ranchers prospered.

The fierce battle of the Alamo in 1836, in which over two hundred men were killed (including early American folk heroes Davy Crockett and Jim Bowie), brought in hordes of Easterners eager to help Texas "Remember the Alamo." The new arrivals were promised land bounties by the Texas legislature: one square mile of land for six months' volunteer military service, two square miles for service of one year. Santa Anna, the Mexican commander, was defeated, and the Territory of Texas became the independent Republic of Texas. In 1845 Texas was admitted to the United States.

TEXAS CATTLE RANCHING

"Many an early Texan lived almost as wholly from his cow as the Plains Indian from his buffalo. She was meat, fat, soap, and candlelight to him, and her skin had even more uses than the buffalo's. Although it was less commonly the white man's dwelling, she often did provide his shelter and the cover for his wagon bows, the door to his first dugout, and perhaps the floor and the rugs. Early ranch and settler shacks were often lined with rawhide against the blue northers and the scorpions, centipedes, and rattlesnakes. Rawhide made the woven bottom of the Texan's springless bed and his chairs, stools, cradles, trunks, valises, baskets, buckets, and dough pans and even the settler's churn, although some thought it gave the butter a peculiar flavor.

"Cowskin furnished the rancher his winter coat, his carriage and wagon robes, and often his bedcovers, as rawhide made his poncho and his chaps, his chaperejos, to protect him against brush and thorns and rain and cold. In addition to the regular leathern uses, rawhide often took the place of iron, cotton, wood, and even silver or paper. It was the rawhide riata in place of the surveyor's chain that measured off the Spanish land grants. The horses were hobbled with strips of rawhide instead of iron, and sometimes shod with it, as were the oxen. In a pinch rawhide served as slates, blackboards, playing cards, and faro table tops. Portraits and holy pictures were embossed or burned on it. When the horrifying cholera epidemic of 1849–50 swept up along all the western trails to the edge of swift water, and reached San Antonio, too, there were so many dead in the town and the fear of infection was so great that the corpses were simply rolled into cowhides and buried. To the Texan the cow was all the things the buffalo was to the hunting Indian, except perhaps the center of his highest religious ritual that the buffalo occupied in the sundance of many Plains tribes, and perhaps that could come, too." *

* Mari Sandoz, *The Cattlemen* (New York: Hastings House, 1965).

xxxxxxxxxxxxxxxxxxxxxxxxxxxxxxxxxxxxxxxxxxxxxxxxxxxxxxxxxxxxxxxxxxxxxxxxxxxxxxxxxxxxxxxxxxxxxxxxxxxxxxxxxxxxxxxxxxxxxxxxxxxxxxx

By the time Texas joined the Union, methods of ranching were changing. Cattle ranching no longer combined farming with the raising of cattle but became a separate operation. Influenced by the system of the Mexican *ranchos,* Texans began to adopt the open-range method of cattle raising.

Cattle fever struck Texas much in the same sense that gold fever attracted settlers to California. Those who dreamed of a promised land were very often disappointed, although some did manage to make their fortune. (In 1853 Richard King and a partner bought 15,500 acres of land for $300. The ranch spread out, eventually, to over a million acres.) The range was open, buffalo herds and Indians added zest to the life of the cowboy, and by the early 1850s the first of the cattle trails were established—east to Louisiana, west to California, and north to the Midwest. For three decades prior to the Civil War the burgeoning Texas culture was centered on longhorn cattle, the vast open plains, new ranches, and the search for trails and markets where cattle were to be sold.

It was after the Civil War that the classic trail drives took place. Cattle that had run wild during the war were rounded up and driven north to the railheads that were pushing their way west into Missouri and Kansas. A vast market awaited them there: the crews building the railroads, the towns that grew up alongside, and the eastern market, which could now be supplied by those railroads.

Cattle were driven up and across the public lands, feeding on blue grama and buffalo grass, along trails streaming northward out of southern Texas. The Shawnee Trail, originally established by settlers heading south into Texas, led to Missouri. The Goodnight-Loving Trail, named after a rancher and his partner, was utilized after it was discovered that the western frontiers (in this case, New Mexico) could support cattle; it ran up to Denver and Cheyenne. The Western and Cimarron trails ended at Dodge City. The most-traveled cattle route was the Chisholm Trail, which began at the Rio Grande and headed straight north to Abilene, Kansas.

As the size of these herds grew—often numbering over 2,000 head—the problems grew: quarantine regulations, lands trampled by cattle, and towns overrun with buyers, dealers, and celebrating cowboys. One such cattle dealer was Joseph McCoy, who first saw the small, desolate town of Abilene, Kansas, in 1867. The town had no more than a dozen crude log huts with roofs made of hard dried dirt. But McCoy was inspired; he saw that Abilene was the farthest point east where a good depot for the cattle business could be established. It was here that the first major midwestern beef terminal was created. The Union Pacific Railroad paid McCoy $5 for every carload of steers. He bought 230 acres west of town, ordered pine lumber from Missouri, and built pens for 300 head of cattle. He then distributed handbills all over Texas extolling the hot-shot saloons of Abilene. In the fall of 1867, forty-four cowboys arrived with 2,400 longhorns. Between 1868 and 1871 the Chisholm Trail, which led straight to McCoy's sale yards, handled 1.5 million head of cattle. Joseph McCoy had succeeded in creating a business as well as a western boom town where cattle, cowboy, and townspeople came together.

THE LONE STAR COWBOY

"It is singular why a 'vaquero' or cowboy will attract so much attention here in the east. Why it is I cannot say, but I have noticed this in all places east of the Mississippi river. Most people imagine we are all desperadoes, and think little of putting a bullet into a man at the slightest provocation, but, as a rule, the vaqueros are a good-hearted class of men. They dress roughly, as the nature of their work requires clothing to be made of very strong material; that is why we wear heavy leather overalls called 'chapps.' It is frequent that the boys have to ride on the jump through sage brush, prickly cactus, etc., when searching for stock, and nothing is more endurable than leather. As there are many people in the States who are not familiar with the work we perform, I will describe a few of our many duties.

"A cowboy must rise usually at the first break of day, and not complain of his 'chuck' (food) which day after day consists of fat bacon, coffee, bread and potatoes, and now and then venison. I will describe the round-up, as there are many people who are familiar with the name and yet know little about the work we are obliged to perform when taking part in one.

"After a limited breakfast you must be off, and, with your pards, search the country for stock, which has, during the several months of grazing on the ranges, drifted many hundred miles. It should be remembered that cattle belonging to many different owners are allowed to range on the government land, and they thus get intermixed. It will now appear plain that a large number of men are required to round up this stock. The several stock owners unite twice a year, in the fall and spring. We usually separate in small parties, and then ride over the ranges, driving cattle of all hands to some stated point, where, after a large number have been collected, we separate the different brands, and turn them over to their respective owners. This is no easy matter to perform. Then, again, the calves have got to be branded, altered, ears cut, beef cattle separated, and many other duties too numerous to mention here. In trailing cattle to the railroad great care is required in order to get them there in good condition. You must not hurry them to cause foot soreness; you must avoid having a stampede, if so your work for weeks may be thrown away. There are many ways which will cause a stampede. Perhaps when the cattle are herded together at night a thunder storm will come up, and the heavy claps of thunder will terrify your stock, which will cause them to stampede in all directions. Then again the bark of a 'coyote' may start them, or, during the night some may become restless and in getting up tramp on those laying down. Then look out for trouble. It is on such occasions that our duty is of the most dangerous kind. We are obliged to ride after the cattle in the darkness, on our ponies, which have been hastily saddled, over usually a very rough country, not knowing what instant both you and your pony will go down into some hole. The boys ride on the outside of the herd, and by hitting them with our heavy whips and trying to get them to circle, if we are so fortunate as to do so, those cattle in the centre are in time brought to a standstill, and the others, seeing those in the centre stop, gradually get over their fright

and halt also. Sometimes it is impossible to stop them, and the herd scatter in all directions, but few are lost, as they are recovered in the next round up. Possibly after a stampede we are only enabled to get a few hundred head to the railroad, when perhaps our band originally contained several thousand. The above are only a very few of many duties we are called upon to perform. We usually ride and break our own ponies, and to one who has never been on the back of a bucking broncho, my advice is to try it if you have got the nerve, and you will in an instant find that a broncho is far different from the old family horse.

"Before closing I will mention the names given to articles by the cowboys. Horses are called 'cayuses'; saddle girths, 'cinchas'; straps attached to cinchas, 'latigo strap'; unbranded cattle, 'mavericks'; leather coverings over stirrup, 'tapaderoes'; leather bag, 'cantanas'; leather overalls, 'chapps'; rubber coat, 'slicker'; whips, 'quirts'; revolvers, '44 or 45'; horse manglers, 'horse herders'; hats, 'sombreros'; whisky, 'family disturbance'; ranch houses, 'shacks'; teamsters driving cattle, 'bull whackers'; after a heavy fall of snow should the weather moderate and snow rapidly disappear, a 'chinook' is said to have set in. It will take a tenderfoot some years to become familiar with the habits, customs and expressions of the cowboys. Very few young men from the east make good cow-punchers; the life is too uncertain, and dangers too numerous to please them."*

* *The Western Vaquero or Cowboy* by A Broncho Buster, L. F. Foster, The Cowboy Pistol Shot. Copyright by L. F. Foster, 1897.

Cardboard cut-out from Gene Autry Melody Ranch Cut-Out Dolls, *Whitman Publishing Company, 1950.*

The cowboy who headed up the northern trails from Texas after the Civil War was thought of as a new and interesting phenomenon by eastern newspapermen and fiction writers. Though the occupation of cowboy was already three centuries old in America by the late 1800s, it was the long cattle drives from Texas to Kansas that moved writers of the time to create the romance of the cowboy and the Wild West as it is thought of today. That actual time period of the American cowboy was from the end of the Civil War until the mid-1880s. The total number of cowboys riding cattle trails has been estimated at 35,000 to 40,000. American politicians, however, observing the centennial of the Declaration of Independence in Philadelphia at the height of the cowboy era, chose to ignore the life and work of this western hero who was being mythologized in print. There was no presentation of western culture at this celebration. Many of the elite continued to regard the cowboy as just an overworked, dirty laborer—a man who had an overinflated image of himself as a fast-shooting tough guy.

Yet America yearned to hear more and more about the wild western frontier, cattle, and cowboy. Many young Easterners after reading about cowboys in newspaper accounts or dime novels became enchanted by the idea of broad-brim hats, high-heeled pointed boots, spurs, leather chaps, and life on the open range—and ran away from home to try to become cowboys.

The actual word "cowboy" has been traced to first-century Ireland, where horsemen and cattle wranglers were referred to as "cow-boys." Centuries later these Irish "cow-boys" fell into ill favor with the British rulers and were banished to America. American colonists preferred to use the word "cow-keeper" because Loyalists referring to themselves as "cow-boys" stole cattle from American farmers and sold them to the British during the Revolutionary War.

The cowboy was a good and honest worker who remained loyal to his ranch boss. A silent cowboy code, a cowboys' gentlemen's agreement, existed, defining conduct and behavior: A cowboy had to have courage in the face of danger; cowardice could affect a whole ranch outfit. A cowboy had to remain cheerful in attitude even

Postcard showing cowboy in full Early West regalia: chaps, high-heeled boots with spurs, gun belt, neckerchief, hat, and gloves. Copyright 1906, Chicago/White City Art Co.

when tired or sick; complaining was taboo, as it was associated with quitting and a real cowboy never quit. He always had to help a pal or "pard," a stranger, or even enemies in trouble, since mutual help was a necessity for survival on the wide-open range. He was also obliged to do his very best at all times. An attitude of "live and let live" was essential to life on the plains; every man had a right to his own way of

life without interference from others, and unnecessary moralizing was not the stuff of cowboys. A real cowboy did not overinterpret; that was left for religion or for sermonizing intellectuals, who were few and far between. There was a scarcity of women in the early trail days. Cow country was man's country, but as ranching evolved, women became the wives and daughters of ranchmen. A cowboy, as a ranch employee, could show no interest on a social level other than accepting a good meal. A cowboy was obliged to protect decent Christian women and to treat them with respect.

A Cowboy and His Horse

A cowboy was inseparable from his horse—the Western movies are right about that—always taking care of his "best pal," feeding him before he ate his own grub, saddling and unsaddling his horse himself. On the ranch a cowboy could be responsible for eight to fifteen horses, trimming and thinning their tails and shodding their hooves.

On a ranch, a herd of broken or part-broken wild horses was fenced in by the corral. Tough cowboys, "bronc busters," or traveling professional "bronc peelers" rode an undomesticated horse till he stopped kicking. Some cowboys liked to break a bronc just for the fun and thrill of it after a hard day's work. Contests and horse betting, sometimes with whiskey included, would find several yipping cowboys riding a bucking bronc, setting the stage for the western rodeo sport of today.

Sometimes cowboys were known to be cruel to the animals they lived alongside, taking their frustrations and hostilities out on them, twisting and breaking a horse's tail or maliciously rubbing sand in a cow's eyes. A work horse was used like a piece of farm machinery but was also regarded as a member of a rough and tough team. Cowboys themselves were hard workers and sometimes dropped from sheer exhaustion. Horses and cowboys on the range were not unalike; they had a special relationship with each other that a cowboy could not attain with a "dumb" cow. A horse was sensitive to his cowboy rider, just as a cowboy had to understand a horse if he expected him to work.

Life in the Bunkhouse

The cowboy lived in a ranch bunkhouse, where he hung his possessions over his bunk bed—his gun belt, his chaps, and his hat. Ranch bunkhouse life in the nineteenth century was akin to slum life, a battle against filth and boredom. The stench of sweat, dry cow or horse manure, plug or chewing tobacco, old boots, and burning coal-oil lamps created a polluted atmosphere inside the poorly constructed shacks. Walls would be lined with newspapers, magazine pictures, and calendars. Picture books, mail-order catalogues, and medicinal remedy pamphlets were usually strewn about. A ranch was set up more for cows than for the people who inhabited it; and the cowboy had to make do with his ramshackle accommodations.

Time in the bunkhouse was spent mostly in waiting for the call to the open range. Cowboys played cards or dominoes to fill the empty time. A gun would often be used with recklessness as if it were a toy. When boredom became too intense and the tension mounted, a cowboy gone wild would fire random shots at the ceiling to break the monotony. Cowboys liked to curse among themselves, sometimes using the term "sonuva bitch" in every other sentence.

In a lighter mood, sitting around the bunkhouse or in front of an open campfire, cowboys would laugh about eastern manners, habits, and dress, tell tall stories, brag about feats in bronco riding, or sometimes sing songs of the old corral, cattle and buf-

Children's illustrated book with dust-jacket cover art by H. C. and Lucille Holling, Platt & Munk, 1936. "Cowboy" sheet music published by Peter Maurice Music Co., London, 1936.

Cardboard cut-outs from Gene Autry Melody Ranch Cut-Out Dolls, *Whitman, 1950.*

Siesta, *painting by Lon Megargee, reproduced on a postcard, c. 1945.*

falo on the plains, or the wandering ways of cowboys. They enjoyed a good practical joke but could also laugh sadistically when a "greenhorn" was thrown from his horse and broke a limb or even his neck.

A ranch outfit on the range included a cook, a horse wrangler, ten to twenty cowboys, and a wagon boss from whom the others took orders. Horse wrangling was usually the first job for a new cowboy (called a "punk")—rounding up horses several times a day, separating roundup horses from cutting horses, which were highly trained for cutting out cattle from a herd. Between roundups a cowboy's work included feeding stock cows, moving them to pasture, and riding a fence to check for broken wire. Sometimes he would ride the range searching for unbranded calves or cattle that might be injured or sick. Water supplies were checked, bulls were herded, and calves and cows gathered to be shipped for slaughter. The monthly wage for a cowboy in the 1880s and 1890s was approximately $35, while top hands got $45 and trail bosses received about $60. A ranch foreman or wagon boss got the high sum of $125.

"The Cow-Puncher's Bunk,"
photographic postcard, c. 1910.

An Interesting Story, *painting by Reynolds, reproduced on a postcard, c. 1910.*

Above: *Collectible cowboy cigarette card (front), Hassan Corktip Cigarettes, 1910.* Below: *Cigarette card with bunkhouse story (back), Hassan Corktip Cigarettes, 1910.*

DARNING HIS SOCKS

The leisure hours of a cowboy are few. What time is not taken up with the regular work is filled in by many odd duties. Some of the horses that are not completely broken have to be given a few lessons. A good deal of time has to be put in practicing with the rope. Skill in using it is absolutely essential in ranch work. If there is any mending of saddles or bridles necessary, that must be taken care of. About the last thing the cowboy thinks of is looking after his own clothes. His hat, boots and gloves are the best he can buy. The rest he cares little about. There are times, however, when his socks must be mended. This he will attempt with painful effort. A man who can do all kinds of things with a lariat will have great struggles with a darning needle. As the artist has shown, a companion is likely to enliven the performance with his comments.

— • —

COWBOY SERIES
1-50
HASSAN   CORKTIP
                          CIGARETTES
          The Oriental Smoke

THE LARGEST SELLING BRAND OF CIGARETTES IN AMERICA
FACTORY Nº 649 1ST DIST. N.Y.

Jim Williams's Out Our Way *sketches of cowboy life were popular favorites of newspaper readers starting in 1924; this collection was published in 1943, in hardcover with dust jacket, by Charles Scribner's Sons. (P.C.)*

The Chuck Wagon

Roundups began at the ranch, where a roundup boss organized one to ten chuck wagons, depending on the size of the open range and the number of cattle in the herd, each with a cook in charge. Cowboys would move with a chuck wagon out onto the plains to "whoop-up" the cattle for slaughter. Good food and a good cup of coffee around an open fire were part of what attracted a cowboy to a specific ranch, so a cook, or "cookie" as he was called, was seen as a very important element of a ranch team. Chuck wagons carried lineaments, medical supplies, screw-worm remedy for cattle sores, and a tool chest. Food supplies consisted of coffee, salt, soda, cornmeal, beans, sugar, molasses, honey, rice, dry fruit, baking powder, and wheat flour. Utensils were iron pots and pans, and tin plates, cups, spoons, knives, forks, and ladles.

The "cookie," or "beanmaster," had to please the cowboys; a good meal was seen as the just reward for a day's work. Sourdough bread, pancakes, and bacon were breakfast. Since meat and game were readily available, a cowboy's dinner grub was usually rice, beans, and meat with cornbread. Somewhere along the Chisholm and Western trails during the early 1870s, chilies, peppers, and spices from Mexican cooking began to enter into chuck-wagon cooking. Spicing up the meat with hot chili peppers and adding water was the basis of the first chili pot as we know it today. Beans usually were not added to the mix, but the meat might consist of beef, pork,

chicken, armadillo, or even an occasional rattlesnake.

Chili became the "official" dish of Texas and remains so today. A basic early Texas cowboy chili known as "Cowboy Bob's Chili Fixins," which you can make on your own stove, includes:

4 **pounds coarse-cut or chopped meat**
2 **tablespoons fat or oil**
1 **chopped onion**
5 **or 6 minced garlic cloves**
5 **or 6 finely diced hot red or green chili peppers**
2 **to 4 tablespoons hot chili powder**
  Black or white pepper
1 **quart spring water**
1 **tablespoon paprika**
1 **tablespoon crushed cumin seed**
1 **teaspoon Spanish oregano**
1 **teaspoon salt**
1 **teaspoon sugar**
6 **tablespoons flour**
1 **can tomato sauce**
1 **or 2 cans beans**

"The Chuck Wagon—The Cowboy's Kitchen," postcard from an early photograph, c. 1939.

Sear the meat in the melted fat or oil in a large covered iron pot until it turns gray. Add onion and garlic, hot peppers, chili powder, pepper, and spring water. Cover, bring to a boil, add paprika, cumin, oregano, salt, and sugar, and cook over low heat for 45 minutes. To thicken, add flour and a can of tomato sauce. Add the beans, cook another 30 minutes, stir, and serve.

Some cowboys frown on the practice of adding beans. Cowboy chili can be hot, red-hot, or "hotter than hell," depending on the amount of Mexican peppers used. Many chili contests and cook-offs take place today, and recipes abound that add mushrooms, beer, and almost anything you can name; but a basic chili of the Texas plains as described above, though simple, is often the best.

Cattle-trail chili became popular in all the trail towns; and it is said that cowboy outlaws Frank and Jesse James always ate a few bowls of "hot red" prior to a holdup. In Military Plaza in San Antonio, Texas, dozens of chili wagons run by Mexican "Chili Queens" appeared in the 1880s, competing for the cowboys' favor, each with its own individual brand of the Tex-Mex concoction. Their wagons illuminated with brightly colored lanterns, these exotic cooks dished out chili con carne from dusk to dawn to cowboys coming in from the range.

Cardboard cut-outs from Gene Autry Melody Ranch Cut-Out Dolls, *Whitman, 1950.*

Cowboy Wild

As the railroads moved farther west, the cow towns prospered and grew, each becoming known at various times as the Capital of Sin and Violence. These included Ellsworth, Wichita, Dodge City, Ogallala, Cheyenne, Tascosa, Miles City, and Denver.

The cattle pens were followed by the barroom, the theater, the gambling rooms, the bawdy house, or "good time" house, and the dance hall. The first building to go up in a cow town was the saloon. The first cowboy bar was often just a whiskey barrel on a wagon stationed alongside a cow trail. Straight whiskey was drawn right out of the barrel into a tin cup or large tumbler.

Top: *General Foods Log Cabin Syrup, 5-pound syrup tin, litho on metal process, 1940s.* Bottom: *Reverse.*

Thrilling Western "pulp" published by Standard Magazines, March 1946.

Cowboys referred to this barrel brew as "rotgut," "red-eye," or "tarantula juice."

As a cow town grew in size, saloons, as opposed to the church in other towns, continued to be the center of most social life. Entering the traditional swinging doors you would see a long bar, gambling tables on the far side of the room, a large open floor space, and hanging oil lamps. Some of the bars had colorful names: The Bucket of Blood, The Road to Ruin, Golden Grain, Korral Bar, The Oriental Palace, The Lone Star Saloon.

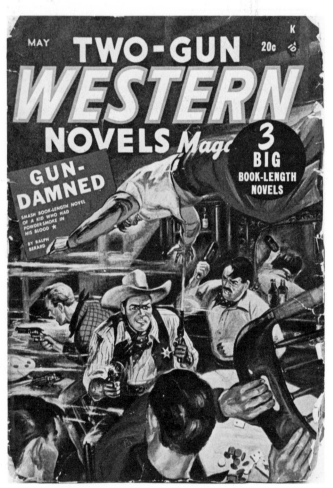

Two-Gun Western Novels Magazine *with cowboy-wild cover art, published by Exclusive Detective Stories, May 1948.*

Working on a ranch or on the range was a rugged man's job; and sometimes after several months of labor on the plains a restless cowboy would yearn (get a hankerin') to hit town. There he would spend his hard-earned cash on liquor, gambling, and women of ill repute. Many townsfolk would look to take advantage of an innocent cowboy on a spree. The cowboy who had saved a little money, say $100, would generally ride off the ranch, head for town, put his horse in a livery stable, check into a hotel, and wander into a saloon, where he would drink and play cards, letting loose sometimes for a week or more before heading back to the ranch. A ranch boss anticipated this pattern; he knew the cowboy had worked hard, felt isolated, built up tension, and needed a binge. Usually these binges would clean him out financially, forcing him back to work on the ranch. Often he took advantage of slow times, particularly in the winter, to run "cowboy wild."

Towns like Abilene attracted this type of cowboy as well as the more innocent types. One cowboy of the day remarked, "We do not think anything of seeing one or two dead men on the streets every morning." Lawmen were required to keep towns under some kind of civil control. Abilene hired James Butler Hickok, the legendary "Wild Bill," a loner type of cowboy who was also a master of two ivory-handled Navy Colts.

By the time Hickok rode into Abilene in 1871, during the town's biggest cattle season, his career as an Indian scout had been a story feature in *Harper's New Monthly.* "Sure am glad to meet you," Hickok would say, "but hand me those guns." One man who refused was immediately shot down by Wild Bill. Setting up his headquarters in the Alamo Saloon, Wild Bill always presided there in a chair with his back to the wall. Cattle fortunes changed hands often

Wild Bill Hickok and Jingle and Wagon Train gun and holster sets, 1950s. Ted Hake collection.

in Abilene, but records show not a single holdup during Wild Bill's nine months in office, though he made several dangerous enemies. In the autumn of that same year the Abilene *Chronicle*'s headline read: AT-TEMPT TO KILL MARSHAL HICKOK. This was one of several attempts to collect a reward of $10,000 that a Texas rancher was said to have offered as revenge on Hickok, who had shot down his son. This rumor fol-lowed Wild Bill to Deadwood, South Dako-ta, where five years later he was shot in the back, dying instantly, by reward-mad Jack McCall.

As the railroad moved westward, other shipping points were established—like the Kansas town of Newton, which had first been settled in 1871. Known as a wild town where sixteen-year-old girls drank, smoked

cigars, and cursed a blue streak, Newton was famous for the Newton Massacre, a shootout between gamblers and Texas cow-boys in which nine men were killed or wounded. Another famous cow town was Ellsworth, also in Kansas, where in 1873 there were 1,000 permanent residents and an equal number of drifters, including about 75 professional gamblers and many more cowboys. Known as a "nasty" place, Ellsworth boasted a bawdy section called "Nauchville."

Dodge City, called "Queen of the Cow Towns" from 1876 to 1885, is still a cattle town. Known as a "money" town, the old Dodge City was without law and order. Dif-ferences were settled by six-shooters or ri-fles. Some of the star officers of Dodge City included Sheriff Bat Masterson, Marshal

Calamity Jane   Wild Bill Hickok

Calamity Jane and Wild Bill Hickok are buried side by side in Mt. Moriah Cemetery in Deadwood, South Dakota. This 1950 "C. T. Art-Colortone" postcard was distributed by Black Hills Post Card Co., Deadwood, South Dakota.

Charlie Basset, and assistants Wyatt Earp and William Tilghman, and the town was known by cowboys and outlaws alike as the place where a Bad Man of the West would meet his equal. Word spread among cowboys that they might wear their six-shooters into town but that they'd better leave them at the first stop—a hotel, livery stable, or business place. A six-shooter was no match for the quick-shot lawmen with their Winchesters and buckshot. The history of Dodge City with its legendary cowboys and lawmen and beautiful entertainers like Dora Hand, who was shot accidentally during a shoot-out at the height of her career as a singer at the Alhambra Saloon, has inspired countless novelists, filmmakers, and television scriptwriters.

One of the most famous characters of the Wild West was "Calamity Jane," whose full name was Martha Jane Canary. She got her nickname from a threat she once made that calamity would befall anyone who opposed her. Calamity Jane liked to wear men's clothes and carouse with the cowboys, but she was not herself an outlaw. Garnering a reputation as an alcoholic who didn't know when to stop, Jane was known in all the saloons throughout South Dakota, Montana, and Wyoming. One of her pet expressions was "a high lonesome," which was a euphemism for a prolonged drinking binge.

The notorious James boys, Frank and Jesse and their younger brothers, were famous outlaws who stole almost half a million dollars from banks and trains and killed twenty-one men between 1866 and 1876. Jesse was killed in 1882; Frank spent his declining years as a farmer. Of them, Nat Love, a nineteenth-century black cowboy said, "Their names are recorded in history as the most famous robbers of the new world but to us cowboys of the cattle country who knew them well, they were true men, brave, kind, generous and considerate, and while they were robbers and bandits, yet what they took from the rich they gave to the poor . . . and if they were robbers, by what name are we to call some of the great trusts, corporations and brokers, who have for years stolen from the people of this country."* Obviously the James boys were the Robin Hoods of the West.

John Wesley Hardin, another symbol of outlaw defiance, was an expert gunslinger and had already murdered eight men by the time he was eighteen. After gunning down a total of more than forty men in his career, mostly blacks, Indians, and Mexicans, Hardin was tracked down by the Texas Rangers and imprisoned for fifteen years. While there, he studied law and wrote his autobiography.

Billy the Kid was born in New York around 1859 and moved westward in the late 1860s. His first murder, the shooting of a blacksmith, was provoked by a harmless insult. Sent to jail, he managed an escape because he had large wrists and small hands, enabling him to slip out of his handcuffs. Later, working as a cowboy, he was involved in the Lincoln County War over range rights. He killed Sheriff William Brady. Jailed again, he escaped once more and soon had his own band of outlaws. Pat Garrett finally cornered him in 1880. Tried and ready to hang, he got away, killing two guards. Garrett trailed Billy to Fort Sumner, New Mexico, and killed him with one shot.

A Daughter of the West

"A Daughter of the West," penny postcard, c. 1900.

Bill Longley hated blacks and killed dozens. When he was captured by Texas lawmen in 1878 and sentenced to be hanged, he chuckled and said, "Hangin' is my favorite way of dyin'!"

Female outlaw Belle Starr was married to the Cherokee renegade Sam Starr. Their ranch was a hideout for desperadoes. Belle planned robberies, sold stolen livestock, and became the image of the glamorous

* The Life and Adventures of Nat Love, New York: Arno Press, 1968.

Bad Woman of the West for generations to come. She was murdered in 1889.

Among the most legendary lawmen of the West was Wyatt Earp, who served as a policeman in Wichita from 1875 to 1876 and as assistant marshal in Dodge City from 1876 to 1879. Later Wyatt joined his brothers Virgil, Morgan, and James in Tombstone, Arizona, along with their pal Doc Halliday, a heavy-drinking tubercular dentist and killer. Virgil was a marshal there; Wyatt dealt faro at a saloon; Morgan rode shotgun on the stage to Tucson; and James was a saloonkeeper. In 1881 a feud developed between the Earp brothers and the Clanton and McLaury brothers, climaxing at the famous O.K. Corral. Wyatt had to leave the area and ended his days quietly in California in 1929.

DON'T FENCE ME IN

In 1862 the federal government granted the West two of its greatest desires: cheap public lands in accordance with the Homestead Act, and the granting of large segments of land to the railroads. In 1869 the first transcontinental railroad was completed, when the Union Pacific from Omaha, Nebraska, and the Central Pacific from Sacramento, California, were linked up at Promontory, Utah Territory. Thousands came to claim their promised 160 acres. Clashes with cattle barons and cowboys followed, cowboys calling the settlers "sod busters" or "nesters." Two other railroads sectioned the country, the Kansas Pacific from Kansas City to Denver (this is the one that the great cattle drives first connected with), and the Atchison, Topeka and Sante Fe from Atchison, Kansas, to Pueblo, Colorado.

The nature of the open range also began to disintegrate with the appearance of barbed wire in the 1870s. The settlers fenced in their cattle and claimed vast amounts of open public land, turning the cowboys into fence cutters. Barbed-wire points cut an animal or a cow worker and violated the cowboy principles. Texas Governor John Ireland held a special session of the state legislature in 1884 in which fence cutting was debated for many long hours. At the end of the session lawmakers made fence cutting a felony punishable by one to five years in prison. This was enforced by the Texas Rangers, and it was the beginning of the end of the open range as it had been known in cowboy country. Barbed wire also stunned the Indians when they saw the endless plains being marked and enclosed by fencing.

The 20 to 60 million buffalo on the western plains were a commissary for the Indians, providing them with food, clothing, and shelter. In the 1870s, with the coming of the railroad, people were encouraged to kill buffalo, even from the moving cars, to provide food for railroad crews and just for the sport. Also, by removing the buffalo, it was reasoned, the Indian commissary would be destroyed. The slaughter of the buffalo between 1870 and the mid-1880s did more than the previous thirty years of fighting to settle the Indian question. In 1880 buffalo in Montana outnumbered steer. Three years later, the buffalo roamed no more.

In 1880 the cattle industry began a five-year boom. A newborn calf cost $5 in Texas and could be fattened for three or four years for nothing on the public lands. Overhead was no more than $5 a steer, figuring in the cost of supplies and horses, salaries of a cowboy worker (about $300 a year), and food costs at 11 cents per cowboy per day. In Omaha a steer sold for $45. The British invested a great deal of money in ranching, as did other nationalities. A Scottish firm, the Espuela Cattle Company, fenced half a million acres and called itself the Spur Ranch. These investments pushed the borders of the open range rapidly northward. Then the cattle market became glutted, forcing prices to sag. Ranches were overstocked, and disaster hit in the form of two harsh, bitter-cold winters in 1885 and 1887, interspersed with droughts. Cattle—as opposed to the stalwart buffalo who stands his ground, head down and into the wind—run in panic from cold weather. In those winters they drifted hundreds of miles, and losses were estimated at 90 percent over wide regions. Bankruptcies followed for many ranchers and stock corporations after those winters. J. Frank Dobie, a noted cowboy chronicler, said, "A whole generation of cowmen were dead broke."

The cowboy age, the buffalo, the Indian, home on the range, the struggle, romance, and glory of the Old West were all at trail's end.

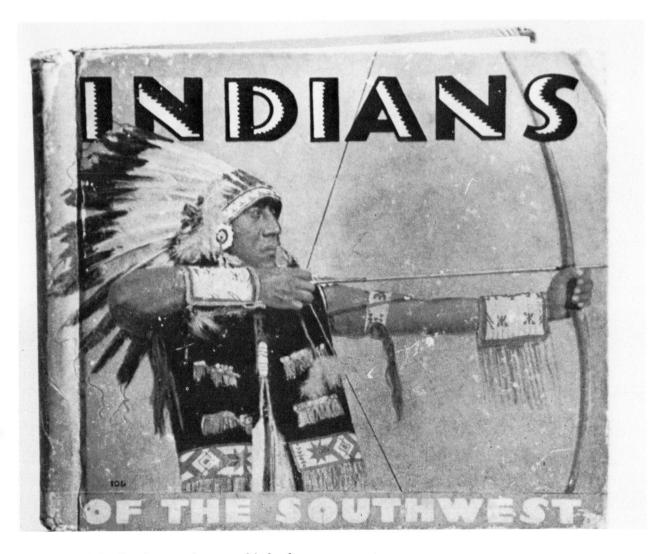

Indians of the Southwest, *photographic book by Harold and Delaine Kellogg, Rand McNally, 1936. (P.C.)*

The Ubiquitous Yank, *Western dime novel, published by*
Arthur Westbrook Co., Cleveland, Ohio, early 1900s.

DIME NOVELS, PULPS,
and COWBOY COMICS

DIME NOVELS
AND PULPS

James Fenimore Cooper's exciting western *Leatherstocking Tales,* along with fictionalized stories of real people such as Kit Carson, Davy Crockett, and Daniel Boone, entered popular American culture before the Civil War in the form of paperback books, which were sold throughout the country for a nickel or a dime.

Maleska: The Indian Wife of the White Hunter, published in 1860 by Beadle and Adams, was the first in that company's series of books issued at the fixed price of 10 cents. Between 1860 and 1898 Beadle and Adams published over 3,000 titles with sales running up to 5 million copies. Ned Buntline, a pseudonym for E. Z. C. Judson, an ex-actor, beggar, jailbird, promoter, drunkard, and temperance lecturer, wrote over 200 novels for Beadle and Adams, most featuring the exploits of William Frederick "Buffalo Bill" Cody. Buffalo Bill also starred in Buntline's play *Scouts of the Plains* in 1872, the beginning of a show-business career, which culminated in

his famous colorful, action-packed, rip-snortin' Wild West Shows.

Buffalo Bill was featured in over 800 dime novels, and in hundreds of others famous cowboys like Wild Bill Hickok, John Wesley Hardin, Billy the Kid, Texas Jack, California Frank, and Bronco Bob and cowgirls like Nan J. Aspinwall ("the Montana Girl"), Alberta Claire ("the Girl from Wyoming"), Belle Starr, and Calamity Jane fixed the image of the Wild West for the entire world. Paul Bunyan, the mythological hero of the old Northwest, was supplanted by Pecos Bill, a southwestern frontier cowboy whose feats included lassoing lightning and riding cyclones and whose rope stretched from the Pecos River to the Rio Grande.

By the turn of the century the basic pattern of the Western story had been set. The first authentic cowboy autobiography, *A Texas Cowboy or 15 years on the Hurricane Back of a Spanish Pony,* had been written by a cowpuncher named Charles A. Siringo in 1885 and was eventually published by five different publishers over a forty-year period. Owen Wister's *The Vir-*

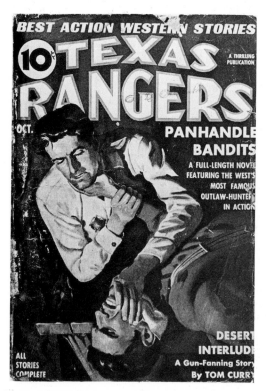

Texas Rangers, *pulp Western stories published by Better Publications, New York, October 1938.*

Lariat, *story magazine of cowboy-life romance featuring a masked black-leather cowgirl avenger, published by Real Adventures Publishing Co., March 1950.*

Frontier Stories, *showing Indian after a blond scalp, published by Fiction House, September 1950.*

Complete Western Book, *pulp Western magazine from Newsstand Publications, May 1938.*

ginian, about Wyoming in the 1880s, was published in 1902 and became the most widely read novel in America. And for everyone who read these books there were thousands more who were reading the dime novels of Ned Buntline, Sam S. Hall, Colonel Prentiss Ingraham, Buffalo Bill himself, and others. The dime novels were published into the 1920s, when they were supplanted by the pulp magazines of Street and Smith, which featured attractive graphic cover art, action-packed short stories and novels, and fictionalized accounts of real events. In 1919 the last of the dime novel publications, the *New Buffalo Bill Weekly,* was replaced with a new pulp called *Western Story Magazine.*

Pulps proliferated in the 1920s and 1930s; in addition to *Western Story Magazine* they included *Argosy, Adventure, Western Trails, Texas Rangers, Star Western, Two-Gun Western, Frontier Stories, Lariat,* and *West.* The better Western novels and stories were published by most major publishers in hardcover in the 1930s, and in the 1940s mass-market Western paperbacks flooded the market.

ZANE GREY AND MAX BRAND

Zane Grey, a New York dentist, published his first novel in 1903 but did not establish a real following until 1912 with *Riders of the Purple Sage,* which sold 1.8 million copies. Grey subsequently wrote fifty-four Westerns, including *The Thundering Herd, The Code of the West, Wanderers of the Wasteland, The Lone Star Ranger,* and *The Vanishing American.* His publishers claimed on the dust jackets of his novels that "the wild fierce blood of Indian chiefs flows in his veins . . . all his stories are splendidly American, thrillingly romantic, packed with action and color."

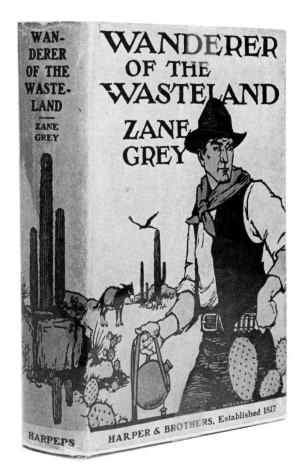

Above: *Cowboy collectible: Zane Grey's* Wanderer of the Wasteland, *illustrated by W. Herbert Dunton, dust jacket by W. Woodruff, published by Harper & Brothers, 1923. First edition.* Below: *Comic-book version of Max Brand's* Silvertip *series from Dell Comics, 1953. (P.C.)*

Another writer, Frederick Faust, who wrote under the pen name of Max Brand and at least ten other pseudonyms, was inspired by Zane Grey's realistic fiction but wrote with a romantic view of the Old West as a land of fable and legend. Brand's first action-packed Western, called *The Untamed* and published in 1919, was a great success. Tom Mix later starred in the silent film version. In 1920 Brand agreed to supply Street and Smith's *Western Story Magazine* with a million words for an indefinite period. He was paid the premium price for pulp writers—5 cents a word—and over a fourteen-year period he wrote 13 million words of Western fiction, earning $100,000 a year from his widely read work. Known as the "King of the Pulps,"

Max Brand created his most famous Western hero in a serial first published in 1930 by *Western Story Magazine. Destry Rides Again* became the all-time Western classic, selling millions of copies over the years. It was Tom Mix's first talkie, provided James Stewart and Audie Murphy with starring movie cowboy vehicles, and even became a Broadway musical with Andy Griffith and Dolores Gray.

BIG LITTLE BOOKS

In the 1930s Whitman Publishing Company began issuing Western novels in the form of the Big Little Books, which were predecessors to the comic book of the

Cowboy Stories, *Big Little Book, with illustrations by Hal Arbo, c. 1935. Introduced many Depression-era kids to the Western novel. Whitman.*

1940s. Other companies issued books in the same format with series titles such as Nickel Books, Penny Books, Top Line Comic Books, and Fast Action Books (which are noted for their exceptional comic artwork on the cover and the inside pages). Saalfield published a series of small books featuring still photographs from the Western movies of Tom Mix, Buck Jones, and others. The actual Big Little Book is 3¾" to 4" wide and 4½" high. It runs about 300 to 460 pages, with the left-hand page containing the text and the right-hand page consisting of a drawing illustrating the text. Initially, Big Little Books (later they were called Better Little Books and New Better Little Books) consisted of novelized newspaper comic strips such as *Buck Rogers, Flash Gordon, Little Orphan Annie,* and *Dick Tracy,* but they soon branched out and included biographies, classics, and movie treatments. Many titles are listed in the sections featuring Gene Autry, Tom Mix, Roy Rogers, the Lone Ranger, Buck Jones, Ken Maynard, Tim McCoy, and Red Ryder. Other Big Little Books with a Western theme include:

Arizona Kid on the Bandit Trail
Big Chief Wahoo
Billy the Kid
Bobby Benson
Boss of the Chisholm Trail
Bronc Peeler
The Lone Cowboy
Broncho Bill
Buffalo Bill
Cowboy Lingo
Cowboy Stories
Dixie Dugan Among the Cowboys
Shooting Sheriffs of the West
Tex Thorne Comes Out of the West
Trail of the Lonesome Pine
Wells Fargo
Western Frontier
Westward Ho

Above: A *"C. T. Art-Colortone"* comic postcard with two very different cowboys, Sanborn Souvenir Co., Denver, c. 1940. Below: *"C. T. Art-Colortone"* dude ranch comic series postcard featuring rodeo cowboys turning on their charm for a cute cowgirl, c. 1940.

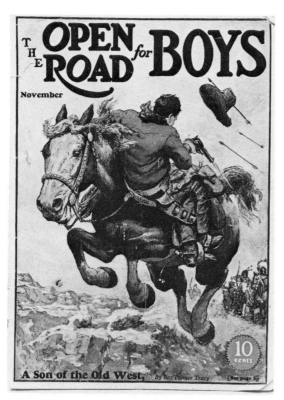

The Open Road for Boys, an adventure magazine for young men, Open Road Publishing Co., November 1931. James Cody Ferris wrote a series of these Western novels for boys and "all who love mystery, rapid action and adventures in the great open spaces." The X Bar X Boys with the Secret Rangers was illustrated by J. Clemens Gretter and published by Grosset & Dunlap, 1936.

PAPER COLLECTIBLES

Tear sheets from the actual comics pages of yesteryear's newspapers are good examples of popular comic art and can usually be found at markets that specialize in paper memorabilia, such as the comic conventions held practically every month in New York and other large cities. At these shows you can buy Sunday comics, song sheets, advertising signs on cardboard (and metal), bubble-gum cards, comic books, movie posters, lobby cards, 8″ x 10″ movie glossies, movie magazines, and postcards. There are special postcard collector clubs, and meetings for trading and buying and selling are held regularly. Postcard collecting is still in the hobby category as opposed to the bona fide antique category, and early cowboy postcards are still obtainable at reasonable prices. Amusement park penny-arcade postcards of your favorite "B" cowboys and cowgirls are quite cheap.

Original art from the "golden age of graphics"—pulp cover paintings, Sunday or daily comic art, paperback book art, and comic-book art—is extremely difficult to obtain, as it was considered expendable when it was produced, and much of it was destroyed. Auction houses are beginning to have special sales for this category of collecting. The next best thing to the original art is the product itself—the pulps, Big Little Books, coloring books, novels, posters, and advertisements—all of which can be found by the Western collector at flea markets, antique shows, comicons, special postcard meets, bookstores, antique shops, and movie specialty shops.

Pulps and paperbacks are collectible today primarily for their exceptionally well-executed action-packed covers, but a pulp with a story by the popular writer Luke Short, a novel by Zane Grey with a dust jacket, or an early paperback with pop-cowboy graphics and a story by Max Brand would also be a lucky find. Edgar Rice Burroughs's Western novels are rare and include *The Deputy Sheriff of Comanche County* (1940), *Apache Devil* (1933), and *The Bandit of Hell's Bend* (1925). Whitman hardcover books are highly collectible, particularly if they are the illustrated books of the movie cowboys Gene Autry, Roy Rogers, and the Lone Ranger.

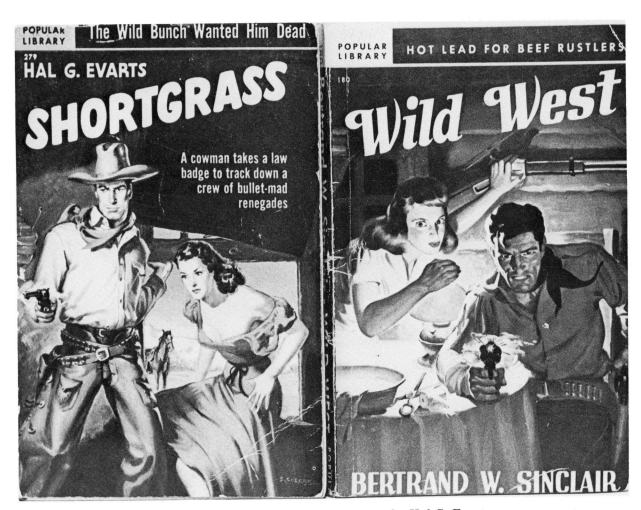

Two Popular Library paperbacks: Shortgrass, *by Hal G. Evarts, 1950;* Wild West, *by Bertrand W. Sinclair, 1946.*

THE BUFFALO BILL STORIES

A WEEKLY PUBLICATION

STORIES

DEVOTED TO BORDER HISTORY

Issued Weekly. By Subscription $2.50 per year. Entered as Second Class Matter at New York Post Office by STREET & SMITH, 238 William St., N. Y.

No. 174.

Price, Five Cents.

BUFFALO BILL'S DOUBLE
OR
THE MEPHISTO OF THE PRAIRIE

BY
THE AUTHOR OF "BUFFALO BILL"

"You devil!" cried Buffalo Bill. "Do what you mean to do. You may be like me in face, but, thank God, we are different in heart and courage."

The Buffalo Bill Stories, *a weekly publication and rare cowboy collectible devoted to border history, September 10, 1904.*

NO BUSINESS
LIKE SHOW BUSINESS

BUFFALO BILL

A major change in the shaping of the mythology of the West was the appearance of the first Wild West Show, which was taken on the road in 1883 by frontier scout and dime-novel hero William F. "Buffalo Bill" Cody and William F. Carver. The show closely paralleled the rodeos, which were first organized as competitions for cowboys at western roundup celebrations. Bronco roping and riding were an aspect of Cody's first three-hour extravaganza, as were feats of marksmanship and the acting out of exciting frontier events, including battles with Indians and stagecoach burnings. Buffalo Bill's success with his Wild West Show inspired others (Charles H. Tompkins Real Wild West Show, 1910) to jump on the Wild West bandwagon trail.

Cody, having been mythologized in the popular dime novels and in plays that greatly exaggerated his frontier feats, scoffed at the Buffalo Bill fictionalization, but he was shrewd enough to exploit it in his shows. He had personally helped the legends by appearing in plays about his ex-ploits and, in 1879, by publishing his memoirs, titled *The Life of Hon. William F. Cody, Known as Buffalo Bill, the Famous Hunter, Scout and Guide: An Autobiography.* He hired real cowboys, dressing them in ten-gallon hats, fur chaps, polished boots, and shiny spurs—a far cry from old ranch-hand cowboy outfits. Easterners seeing the show got the impression that life on the range was one big party filled with the sports of rope twirling and bronc riding. Attractions included mounted Sioux Indians with bright war-painted faces who "whooped it up" to the sound of a cowboy band. Other star attractions included Little Annie Oakley, a cowgirl sharpshooter, Sitting Bull, the Sioux Indian chief who had assisted Custer to his doom, and others. Sitting Bull sold photographs of himself and was known as the "Indian Waxworks" because of his immobile, expressionless face.

The Buffalo Bill Wild West Show—with horses, herds of elk and buffalo, and sixty Indians—earned $100,000 in 1885 and much more during runs at Staten Island and at Madison Square Garden, where it

Cowgirl with Buffalo Bill's Wild West Show, postcard, c. 1908.

attracted over a million people. Famous followers of the show included Mark Twain, P. T. Barnum and Queen Victoria herself. The troupe was invited to celebrate Victoria's Golden Jubilee in London in 1887. Touring for nearly three decades in the States and on the continent, the show reinforced the myth of the American West for the entire world.

BUFFALO BILL COLLECTIBLES

These include posters, advertising cards, newspaper and magazine articles, specialty magazines, programs, postcards, books, sheet music, documents, calendars, tobacco cards, original photos of famous performers like Buffalo Bill or Sitting Bull, cigar-box labels (there was a Jesse James cigar), and other related items. The Buffalo Bill Historical Center in Cody, Wyoming, has been called one of the finest repositories in existence of nineteenth-century Buffalo Bill artifacts. There are also many pop-culture items on Buffalo Bill, including three Big Little Books *(Buffalo Bill and the Pony Express, Buffalo Bill Plays a Lone Hand, The Wild Adventures of Buffalo Bill)*, coloring books, and children's novelized stories of the West.

Colonel W. F. Cody—postmarked North Platte, Nebraska, Buffalo Bill's hometown, 1935.

Getting hold of one of the original Beadle and Adams dime novels, or one of Smith and Street's Log Cabin Library titles (Beadle's competitor), would be very difficult today; they have been highly prized by collectors since the 1920s. For the record, some of the Buffalo Bill titles are:

Buckskin Braves
Road-Agent Round-Up
Death Charm
Royal Flush
Double Dilemma
The Three Bills, Buffalo Bill, Wild Bill and Bandbox Bill or *The Bravo in Broadcloth*
Buffalo Bill's Beagles or *Silk Lasso Sam*
Buffalo Bill Baffled or *The Deserter Desperado's Defiance*
Buffalo Bill's Boys in Blue or *The Brimstone Band's Blot-Out*
Buffalo Bill's First Trail or *Will Cody, The Pony Express Rider*
Buffalo Bill's Winning Hand or *The Masked Woman of the Colorado Canyon.*

CINEMA COWBOY

The first Western film was *Cripple Creek Barroom,* produced by the Edison Company in 1898. This was nothing more than a vignette, but it paved the way in 1903 for Edwin S. Porter's *The Great Train Robbery,* made near Dover, New Jersey. This was the model for future Westerns, giving audiences the illusion of authenticity and the feeling that a great era that had passed could be vicariously experienced on film. Many in the audience fainted and screamed during initial viewings of *The Great Train Robbery.*

The Western very quickly became one of the most popular forms of entertainment. One of the earliest film companies, called Essanay, was formed by G. M. Anderson,

who also became famous as the original cinematic western hero, "Broncho Billy." Broncho Billy, sometimes called the father of all Westerns, made films in Niles Canyon near San Francisco in order to get far enough away from competitor Thomas Edison and to obtain the natural light of the West for his movie making. Broncho Billy added the necessary ingredient—the western cowboy hero star—that the earliest silent Westerns lacked. He acted in over 375 half-hour shorts while head of his Essanay Studios from 1907 to 1917, among them *The Golden Trail* and a host of other weekly serials with Broncho Billy in the title, such as *Broncho Billy's Last Spree*—all adaptations of the dime novels.

Not until Thomas H. Ince and D. W. Griffith entered the filmmaking field did the true Western with more than a basic fast-action plot come of age. Griffith de-emphasized plots in favor of character in *The Goddess of Sagebrush Gulch* and *The Squaw's Love.* Noted Griffith Westerns also include *The Last Drop of Water* and *Fighting Blood* (both 1911) and *The Battle of Elderbush Gulch* (1913).

Thomas Ince, with an Indian star named William Eagleshirt, created a two-reel tragic Western called *The Heart of an Indian,* which presented pioneers and Indians as equals trying to make a living off the land, hunting buffalo and tilling the soil. In 1911 Ince, bored with the cheap budget horse-opera concept of Westerns, hired the entire Miller Brothers 101 Ranch Wild West Show, a group with a large entourage of cowboys, horses, wagons, buffalo, and cattle, to make *War on the Plains,* which was praised for its authenticity as well as its artistic integrity. Other popular Ince Westerns were *Battle of the Redmen, The Indian Massacre,* and *The Woman* (1913), the story of an opera diva with an invalid husband who goes West only to become a saloon singer to be pawed over by drunken cowboys. She becomes a bigamist by marrying a wealthy gambler, but on hearing of her husband's death, she kills herself, leaving behind a suicide note begging for understanding and forgiveness. This was typical of the melodramatic plot lines of silent action films.

EARLY FILM COLLECTIBLES

Collectibles from the era of the silent and early Western talking pictures would fall into the category of movie memorabilia. This encompasses movie posters, lobby cards, autographs, publicity stills, sendaway studio glamour portraits, movie magazines, studio yearbooks, studio promotional material, slot-machine postcards, movie-star cigarette advertising cards, movie-star games, coloring books, novelized versions of motion pictures, scrapbooks, song sheets and song folios, movie programs, gum cards, matchbook advertising, and other paper memorabilia.

It should be noted that paper items are among the most desirable collectibles today. Collectors are advised to pay attention to the litho process, the ink, the type and age of the paper, and, particularly, the condition of the paper when they are dealing with graphics of this kind. Paper-collector newsletters and movie-memorabilia shops abound in most major cities today; and most reliable dealers will authenticate posters or pictures as to their date of issue. Movie posters from a second or third release of a film are not as valuable as ones from the first release. Original studio pictures of stars have been reproduced by the millions; it takes an experienced eye to spot an original (quality and age of paper, certain markings, print process, etc.). Movie posters also are being reproduced, but most Western movie posters are still authentic. Big Little Books or novelized movie books, of course, are always dated, and usually there is a telltale discoloration or yellowing of the paper.

William S. Hart

Griffith and Ince were both forerunners who enhanced the Western film, but it was Ince who signed William S. Hart to a contract. William Surrey Hart helped to change the direction of the Western, rescuing it from mediocrity and bringing to it a rugged realism and authentic poetry. His sense of the integrity of the West, and what he brought to it as an early cowboy hero-actor, created the classic epic-style Western that ultimately became a tradition in Hollywood filmmaking.

Hart's first professional stage role was in *Romeo and Juliet* in his hometown of Newburgh, New York. He achieved recognition as Messala in the original company of *Ben Hur* in 1899, but after a number of seasons with this show his acting career suffered a decline. During this lean period he shared a room with another struggling performer, Thomas Ince. Hart's stage career took an upward turn when he was hired to play a western character named Cash Hawkins in *The Squaw Man*. He followed that success with starring roles in *The Virginian* and *The Trail of the Lonesome Pine*. Later on the road with *The Trail of the Lonesome Pine,* he saw his first Western movie and became obsessed with the idea of making one himself.

When Hart turned up in Los Angeles in 1913 to present himself once again to his old pal Thomas Ince, who had by then become renowned as a filmmaker, he was not given encouragement. Hart at 43 did not seem to Ince to be a bankable star. However, since Ince was riding the crest in the movie business, he decided to give his old friend a chance, and permitted him to help write his own leading roles in two features: *The Bargain* and *On the Night Stage.* Hart left for New York somewhat disappointed by the cowboy life of Hollywood. Thomas Ince discovered after his departure that *The Bargain* was becoming a huge hit in many cities and offered Hart a contract at $125 a week. Hart accepted, learning later that he should have asked for much more. He persuaded Ince to allow him artistic control and as a result he directed most of his own films, including *The Scourge of the Desert, The Darkening Trail, Hell's Hinges,* one of his most famous films, and *The Disciple.*

Hart's gritty authenticity of the open range included using real cowboy outfits and shabby exteriors. His heroes, though outlaws, often came to a happy end, which was a new trend in the early silents, and he set the tone for such "talkie" cowboys as Gary Cooper, Henry Fonda, and John "Duke" Wayne, who owe him a debt as the first "realist" cowboy—focusing on the rough, tough, and ready cowboy as a lone individual confronting the elements and standing for deeper American values of courage, honesty, loyalty, self-reliance, perseverance, and independence of spirit.

Motion Picture magazine featuring a cover painting of William S. Hart by L. Sielke, Jr., June 1917. Kenneth Anger collection.

Hoot Gibson movie magazine picture. Article collection of Jim Hans.

GOOD GUYS AND BAD GUYS

Western stars who followed in the boot prints of William S. Hart in the 1920s were Ken Maynard, Bob Steele, Harry Carey, Buck Jones, Hoot Gibson, Fred Thomson, Jack Hoxie, Leo Maloney, and Tim McCoy.

The assembly-line Western became known as the "B" Western, usually cheaply made according to plot formulas that were pre-established, tried and true with little variation. The star was always a good-guy cowboy who worked with a sheriff tracking down bad-guy cattle rustlers. A chaste romantic female always took second place (even in billing) to the cowboy's horse. The cowboy always rode off on his horse alone into the western sunset in search of new adventure. Often a sidekick went along for the ride, and as "Bs" became double fea-

Hoot Gibson is the typical American cowboy when he 'decks himself out in a checkered homespun shirt, dons a wide, sweeping sombrero and ties a 'kerchief around his neck. Thus attired, he puts fear into the hearts of the ornery hombres

Cardboard movie star lid for ice cream manufactured by Arden Farms in California, 1930s. Sunfreze was the brand for this rare cowboy collectible.

One-sheet poster of Ken Maynard film Boots of Destiny, *Grand National Picture, 1937.*

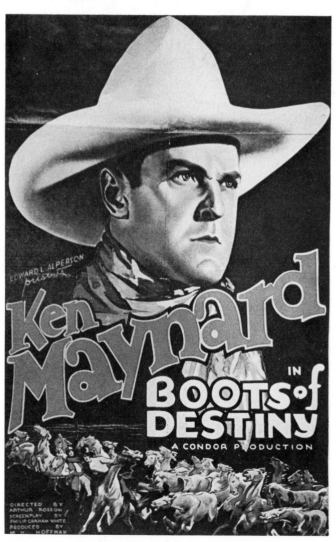

tures in the 1930s and cowboys began to sing on the trail, they were sometimes permitted to ride off with the girl. Mostly it was cowboy, horse, lawmen and outlaws, cattle, Indians, and a bungling comic relief that were included in the "B" Western formula.

Hoot Gibson, who performed for Universal Pictures, was the first comic cowboy to achieve wide acclaim. Comedy with action and intricate stunts were the feature of *The Man in the Saddle, Painted Ponies, The Flaming Frontier* and *The Texas Streak,* all starring the hilarious Hoot.

Fred Thomson, seen by some as rivaling Tom Mix in popularity in the 1920s, helped to incorporate a modern "boy scout" morality into the cowboy myth, influencing many others who followed in the thirties, including Roy Rogers, Gene Autry, and Hopalong Cassidy. Thomson was a former minister who introduced his credo in a film called *A Regular Scout.* He was an expert acrobat and stuntman in films like *The Tough Guy* and *Thundering Hoofs.* His last film, *Jesse James,* was a major Paramount Western and the only one in which the actor died in the end. Ironically, Thomson died just after making the film.

Ken Maynard was another popular star who did his own stunts, performing his own trick horseback riding in a host of epic Westerns for First National, including *Señor Daredevil* and *Red Raiders,* which brought feats of cowboy skill to a new high. Maynard is a legend among old Hollywood cowboys who remember him as a dead shot and an expert horseman who could get out of the saddle of his galloping stallion, Tarzan, pass under his belly, and come up on the other side. When he appeared in the Ringling Brothers Circus he was already known as "The World's Champion Cowboy." Some cowboy cohorts say that he typified the All-American Cowboy. He was hard-drinking, profane, and tempestuous, yet decent, intelligent, and honest. He was disciplined on a ranch, on a horse, making a movie, doing his cowboy thing; but once let loose he was like many other real cowboys before him—bent on running cowboy wild.

Buck Jones made many first-rate Westerns, modeling himself after the rugged style of William S. Hart. His films emphasized realism and authenticity over showmanship, and he was regarded and emulated as a man's man in the 1920s and 1930s, much as cowboys today take their masculine manner from John Wayne. Buck Jones took a tip from Hoot Gibson and employed a touch of comedy in his Fox Westerns. He was also a top stuntman and rider in such films as *Good as Gold, Timber Wolf,* and *The Gentle Cyclone.* Like the Lone Ranger, Buck rode a beautiful white horse named Silver.

Another great host of stars of Western films were not cowboys or their horses, but dogs. Rin Tin Tin led this canine star pack,

Penny arcade penny postcards of Fred Thompson, movie cowboy hero, c. 1920s.

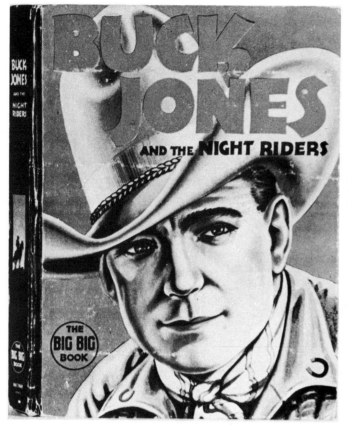

Buck Jones and the Night Riders,
Big Big Book, Whitman, 1937. (P.C.)

*7″ x 5″ studio shot of Frankie Darro,
Buck Jones's sidekick, c. 1935.*

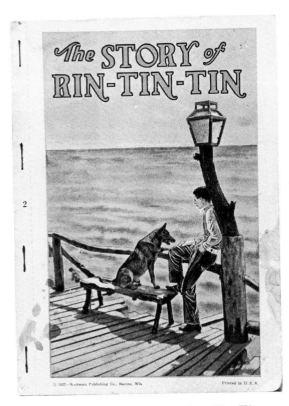

Above: The Story of Rin-Tin-Tin, *a picture book published in 1927 by Whitman.* Top right: *Studio 11″ x 14″ of famous Warner Brothers star Rin Tin Tin, from a promotional campaign book, 1926.* Bottom right: Strongheart, The Story of a Wonder Dog, *by Lawrence Trimble, Whitman, 1926.*

and each studio developed its own dog adventures, with stars named Strongheart, Dynamite, Napoleon Bonaparte, or Peter the Great. Rin Tin Tin was a top moneymaker in the 1920s, and he was regarded as not just a dog that could perform tricks but as an actor who could emote and vary expression and mood with as much expertise as John Barrymore. Famous Rin Tin Tin films for Warners included *Where the North Begins, Tracked by Police,* and *A Hero of Big Snows.*

The cowboys and cowhands who drifted into Hollywood after 1910 in search of gold, glitter, and fame—or perhaps just a

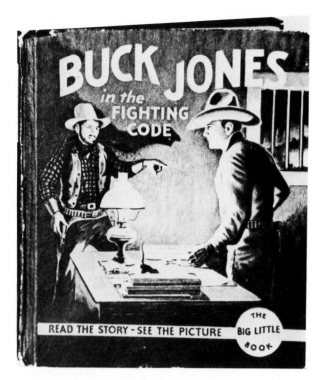

Above: Buck Jones in the Fighting Code, *Big Little Book, Whitman, 1934. (P.C.)* Below: Ken Maynard in Western Justice, *Big Little Book, Whitman, 1938.*

job as an extra or stuntman—were part of the remaking of the West into one of the most potent myths of the American culture. The fantasy it offered became the new western trail wherein legends could be created.

"B" WESTERN COLLECTIBLES

Buck Jones had a radio show called *Hoofbeats,* but it was on the air only for a brief time in 1937 on a syndicated basis. The only premiums offered on his show were a horseshoe pin and ring, a manual and a premium catalogue, and a Jr. Sheriff badge. Buck Jones comics were published by Dell between 1950 and 1952. Buck Jones Big Little Books, mostly published in the middle to late 1930s, include:

Buck Jones and the Rock Creek Cattle War
Buck Jones and the Two-Gun Kid
Buck Jones in Ride 'Em Cowboy
Buck Jones in The Fighting Code
Buck Jones in The Fighting Rangers
Buck Jones in The Roaring West
Buck Jones in Rocky Rhodes
Buck Jones in Red Riders
Buck Jones in Six-Gun Trail

Buck, Tim McCoy, and Raymond Hatton team up in the Big Little Book *The Rough Riders,* and *Buck Jones and the Night Riders* was published as a Big Big Book in 1937.

Ken Maynard was a popular Big Little Book cowboy. His titles include:

Ken Maynard in Gun Justice
Ken Maynard and the Gun Wolves of the Gila
Ken Maynard in Western Justice
Ken Maynard in Western Frontier
Ken Maynard in Six-Gun Law
Ken Maynard and the Strawberry Roan

Buck Jones and Ken Maynard's only co-hort in Big Little Book territory was Tim McCoy. His titles were:

Beyond the Law
The Prescott Kid
The Westerners
The Tomahawk Trail
The Sandy Gulch Stampede

All the cowboys were featured on Dixie Cup ice cream lids throughout the 1930s, 1940s, and into the 1950s.

WILL ROGERS

Perhaps one of the most famous and beloved of all modern cowboy heroes who rode the show business trail into the very heart of America was Will Rogers. He is as much a national institution as Teddy "Cowboy" Roosevelt, Buffalo Bill, or Daniel Boone.

Will Rogers captivated American audiences on stage and in film with his comic gift of gab and cowboy wit, commenting on the events of the day, politics, gossip, and morality with the common horse sense of an old western character. Will Rogers symbolized for people everywhere a humanitarian's view of life as seen from the point of view of the Old West, expansive and with an understanding of the folly and persistent bungling of men.

Rogers's illustrious cowboy career began on the Oklahoma range "punching" cattle but wound up in Zach Mulhall's Wild West Show. He was presented at the old Madison Square Garden as the show's star roper, and Lucille Mulhall (Zach's daughter) was billed as the first woman rodeo performer. Rogers gained notoriety during this New York stint when a steer in a roping event ran wild and jumped over a fence into the terrified, screaming audience. Will, seeing the charging cow, threw out his lariat and roped the animal that had crowds running in panic. The following day Will Rogers found himself being portrayed as a real cowboy hero on the front pages of the New York newspapers, and he decided to remain in the big city when the Wild West show left town, to try his hand at vaudeville.

"Will Rogers and Company" played the vaudeville circuit at modest wages for five years. During this time Will did little talking on stage. Somewhat the shy cowboy, he saved most of his wisecracks and practical jokes for off-stage or "in the wings" banter. However, somewhere along the line he learned that he could get a laugh and that good stand-up comics earned more than a cowboy act in vaudeville. By 1912 he had perfected his cowboy humor and ability to make jokes about what he saw happening or read in the papers, to the delight of his audiences. The following season he was successfully doing a forty-five-minute monologue, in contrast to the usual twelve-minute vaudeville turn.

Rogers was later engaged by Flo Ziegfeld for the Ziegfeld Follies of 1914. "My little old act with the lasso was just put in to kill time while girls were changing costumes," Will said after entering the show. Ziegfeld, an elegant man with cultivated European tastes, was initially repulsed by Will Rogers's vaudeville cowboy humor, but he eventually saw that there was a deep sophistication, albeit a homespun philosophy, underneath those wisecrack puns and commentaries. Rogers and Ziegfeld became lifelong friends, and in the end it was Rogers who helped a down-and-out Ziegfeld, just as he had been helped by him at the beginning of his career. In the Ziegfeld Follies of 1917 Will appeared with blackfaced Broadway newcomer Eddie Cantor and a red-nosed W. C. Fields. So popular did Rogers become that he broke the Ziegfeld rule by being billed ahead of the Follies itself: "Will Rogers in the Ziegfeld Follies."

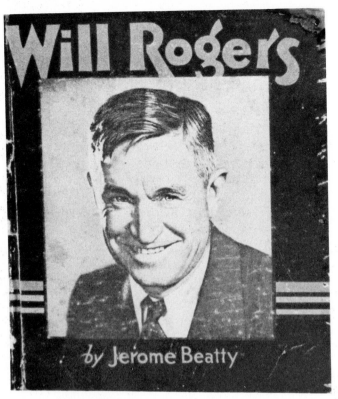

Above: The Story of Will Rogers, *by Jerome Beatty, a pocket-size illustrated five-and-ten book, Saalfield Publishing, 1935. (P.C.)*
Below: *"Vaya con Dios," Will Rogers funeral souvenir program signed by W. S. Hart and Harry Carr, one of 200 copies, 1936. Kenneth Anger collection.*

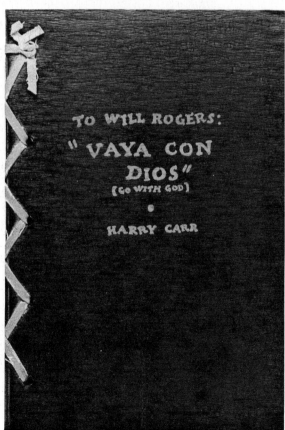

Though his silent films made money, it was as a "talking cowboy" in sound films that Will Rogers became a bankable star and top box-office attraction. Fox Films produced *They Had to See Paris,* a "talkie," in 1929, saw a $700,000 profit, and put Will back to work immediately. Other successful films were *A Connecticut Yankee,* a modernization of the Mark Twain story, *Young as You Feel, Judge Priest, Steamboat Round the Bend, Doubting Thomas,* and *In Old Kentucky.*

Will Rogers's opinions were also to be found in 350 daily and 200 Sunday newspapers coast to coast, with 40 million readers. This column sometimes got Will or his newspaper into hot water when Rogers's tongue-in-cheek jests were misconstrued by the public to reflect the opinion of the paper.

Charles Lindbergh's solo flight across the Atlantic in 1927 in the single-engine plane "Spirit of St. Louis" caught hold of Will Rogers's sense of adventure and pioneering spirit. Aviation became a second career. He admired ace aviators like Lindbergh, Amelia Earhart, Admiral Richard E. Byrd, and the many other men and women who were charting a new frontier in the sky. One of these, Wiley Post, a master aviator, became his skyward-bound mentor. On a vacation jaunt in August 1935, the two men took off from Fairbanks, Alaska, against the advice of Joe Crosson, a hero of several Arctic flights, who wanted them to remain grounded until the weather was less hazardous. On August 15, Rogers and Post crashed in their plane; they were found, both dead, by an Eskimo seal hunter. America mourned Rogers as its national cowboy folk hero just as it had mourned Rudolph Valentino, the greatest lover of the silver screen, almost a decade before. Eddie Cantor said Will was the most popular man of his time. President Roosevelt remembered him as an old friend, a humorist, and a philosopher beloved by all. Will Rogers had been called an American Ambassador of Good Will and a Prince of Wit and Wisdom; millions mourned the passing of a man who seemed to symbolize America itself.

A book called *To Will Rogers: Vaya con Dios* (Go with God), published in 1935 by Angelus Press in Los Angeles and now a rare collector's item, is a letter of farewell to Will from his old pals William S. Hart and Harry Carr. Hart said in this tribute: "When you went away there was more writ about you an' your trip than there was ever writ about any man in the whole world." Harry Carr wrote: "This will seem an emp-

ty world without Will Rogers. To me to face the day without the guidance of his philosophy will be like a ship setting forth without a chart. I depended upon him to bring sweetness and balance and sanity into crisis which to the rest of us seemed angry sores. After every psychic smash that threatened—and happened—I waited for the echo from him."

The echo—the voice of this great American Dream Cowboy Will Rogers—is still reverberating in the land that loved him and that he loved back with so much good humor and sound wisdom. He is certainly one cowboy that will always be remembered, a myth to be treasured and passed on from generation to generation.

He Lit the Genial Fires of Friendship, *reproduced from the original painting by Hector E. Serbaroli. Will Rogers on the cover of a 1944 Christmas calendar.*

TOP BOX-OFFICE BUCKAROO

Tom Mix, the first "King of the Cowboys," was born on January 6, 1880, in Mix Run, Pennsylvania. During his film career, Mix's press agents claimed in a carefully constructed biography that he was born in Texas; that he had fought in the Spanish-American War with the Rough Riders, in the Philippines, in the Boxer Rebellion in China, in Mexico, and in the Boer War in Africa; that he had worked as a ranch foreman, as a Texas Ranger, as a sheriff and as a United States marshal; and that he had become a rodeo champion and been wounded forty-seven times.

Not all the claims have been substantiated, and some have been contradicted in various biographies. However, the facts as we know them are that he *was* born in Pennsylvania (where they have a Wild West Tom Mix Festival every year), and that he enlisted in the army after war was declared on Spain in 1898 but never saw action. Later he went to Oklahoma where he worked as a physical fitness instructor, as a bartender, and as a rodeo cowboy for the Colonel Zack Mulhall Wild West Show, where he met another intrepid performer, Will Rogers. In 1906 he moved from the smaller Mulhall show to the well-organized and well-financed show of the Miller Brothers and their 101 Ranch near Ponca City, Oklahoma. Athletic and superbly conditioned, Tom Mix excelled at hard ranch and rodeo work and became a champion-class rodeo contestant and fine roper.

In 1909 Mix was hired as a stock handler and given a featured part in the saddle-bronc segment of a semidocumentary film called *Ranch Life in the Great South West*. Although the film's purpose was to show how beef cattle were raised and marketed, audience reaction to Mix's fancy shooting and trick riding convinced Colonel William Selig's Polyscope Movie Company to make other one- and two-reel films for distribution to the silent-movie theaters across America, where the Saturday afternoon kids' matinees were proving a lucrative market. Mix made dozens of shorts for Selig-Polyscope, and when they went out of business in 1917 he signed a contract with the William Fox Studios. He had served a good apprenticeship at Selig and was ready for the big-time film industry just when they needed a new cowboy image to replace the aging and overly dramatic William S. Hart.

By 1922 Tom Mix was making $17,000 a week. He never drank or smoked on screen, and he always played fair with the villains, killing only a very few. He also insisted on doing all his own stunts: spectacular leaps over 30-foot chasms, complicated rope swings, wild rides, and rip-roaring brawls. He trained his own stunt horses, which could untie knots and perform amazing leaps and other feats never seen before on screen. Old Blue, the first, was followed by three different "Tonys"—Tony the Wonder Horse (later called Tony Sr.), Tony Jr., and Tony II. Tony Sr., who starred in his own picture, *Just Tony,* for Fox in 1922, knew twenty different tricks and achieved stardom the hard way, jumping over walls and fences, galloping through fire, leaping wide chasms, and plunging off steep cliffs into rivers. Ordered by his master to go to a table and pick up a piece of paper, a hat, a pair of gloves, or a revolver, he did so. He'd drag Tom to safety, stamp upon villains, and jump through plate glass windows. He also had an "understanding" vocabulary of more than 500 words. Tom Mix said that he believed the greatest trick Tony ever pulled was swimming into a flood-swollen river, grasping the handle of a basket supposedly containing a baby, and swimming back to shore. The only thing Tony was afraid of was a dummy horse

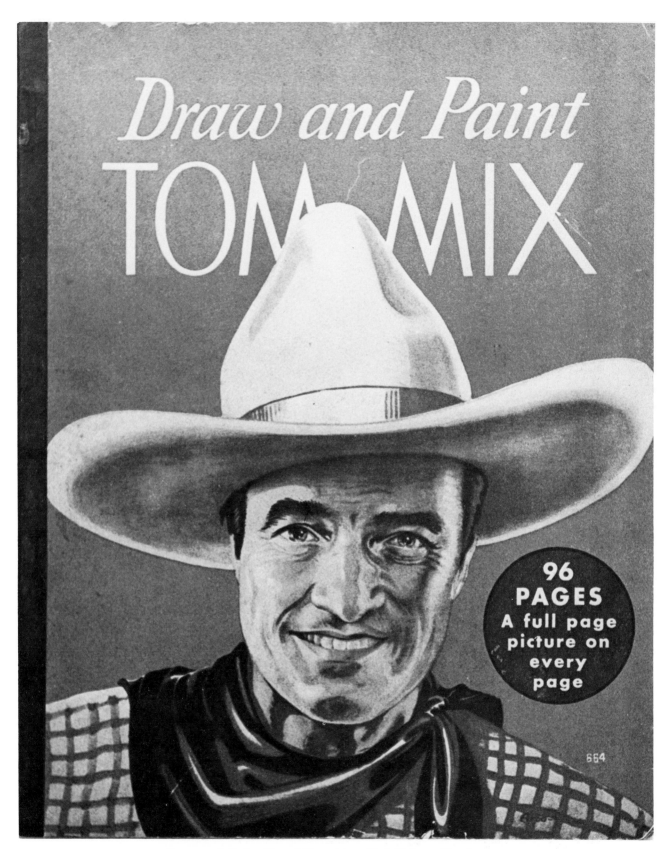

Draw and Paint Tom Mix, *1930s. Ted Hake collection.*

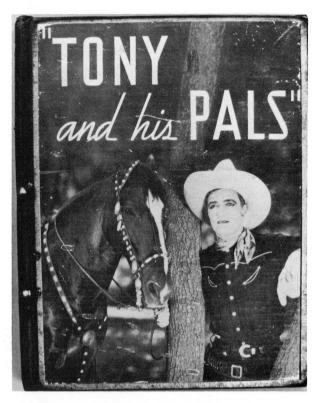

Tony and His Pals,
hardcover published in 1934.
Ted Hake collection. (T.H.)

used by the movie studios, an animal that looked like a horse but wouldn't neigh back or move. Tony, who helped his partner earn $7,500,000 in paychecks over two decades, and had been purchased by Mix in 1909 for $12.50, was the most popular horse in the world. Press agents poured out stories about the special relationship between Mix and his horse, and in an era when horses were becoming less important the stories had wide appeal, increasing Mix's prestige at the box office. Tom and Tony were inseparable, even at personal appearances. The horse even had his own room in a Detroit hotel when Tom discovered that under an archaic law the management was compelled to give shelter to "man and his beast."

While he was with the Fox Studio, Tom Mix established himself as a leading box-office attraction and the number-one cowboy star of the silent screen with such films as *Rough Riding Romance, The Speed Maniac, Treat 'Em Rough, A Ridin' Romeo, Chasing the Moon, Do and Dare, Riders of the Purple Sage, The Rainbow Trail, The Arizona Wildcat, The Last Trail, Hello Cheyenne, Horseman of the Plains,* and *The Great K and A Train Robbery.*

With his experience in the Wild West shows and his years with the Selig-Polyscope Company, Tom Mix knew every phase of the filmmaking industry and is credited with many pioneering innovations. One of these was Mixville, located between Hollywood and the beach at Santa Monica. Cowboys who were appearing in Mix films lived in bunkhouses and cottages on this estate, which included a frontier village, each building fully furnished and suitable for location filming: a saloon, livery barn, assayer's office, etc. He also kept cattle and horses there as well as his large collection of stagecoaches, covered wagons, and buggies, said to have been the best in the West.

In 1925 Mix went on a grand tour of the United States and Europe. Entraining from Hollywood aboard the MixSpecial, he took his wife, daughter, mother-in-law, press agents, family attendants, and grooms for Tony. One baggage car was turned over to his lavish wardrobe. His arrival in New York was tumultuous. Thousands lined the street to catch a glimpse of Tom Mix riding his famous horse Tony. When he boarded the SS *Aquitania* as a first-class passenger, he rode Tony up the gangplank. They walked the decks together during the crossing. The lord high mayors of Southampton, Brighton, and Howe were there to meet Tom and Tony as they debarked in England, presenting Mix with keys to the cities, limousines, and a band escort. In London he stayed in a Hyde Park hotel, and Tony was stabled with the Prince of Wales's horses. They rode together in Hyde Park and were a sensation with the usually staid British public. In Paris, and later in Amsterdam, Berlin, and other cities in Europe, Tom Mix and Tony were hailed as America's greatest ambassadors of goodwill. When he returned to the United States, Mix visited Calvin Coolidge at the White House and Henry Ford in Detroit and made appearances in Boston, St. Louis, and Denver before returning to Hollywood, where he was welcomed back by

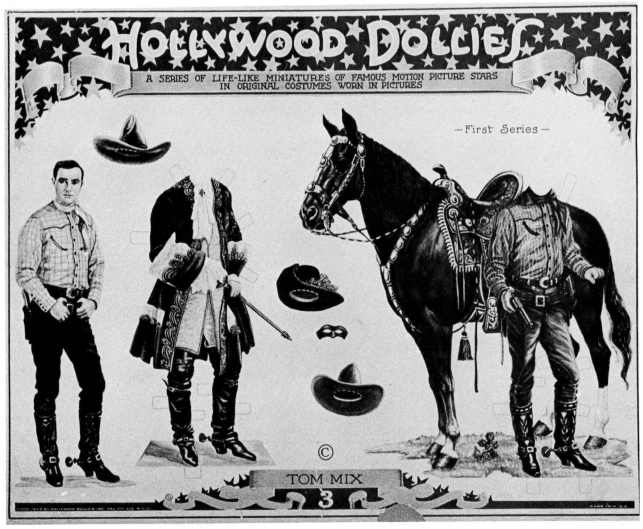

Tom Mix Hollywood Dollies, *1925. Ted Hake collection.*

thousands. Tom Mix's tour had brought international attention and publicity to the Western film and Hollywood. *Variety* labeled him "the greatest cowboy America ever produced."

In 1928 Fox Studios announced the end of silent filmmaking. They were cutting back on Westerns, emphasizing flappers and playboys and drawing-room comedies. Tom Mix recalled his last day at Fox: "I simply nodded acceptance, shook hands with all those men, we had done a lot together, walked out to the stable, saddled up Tony, and rode off the lot. . . . I never wanted to return."

In 1929 he made six pictures for the Film Booking Office (FBO Pictures, run by Joseph Kennedy), but they were not successful. After he lost a reported $1 million in the stock-market crash, including his palace in Beverly Hills and his Arizona ranch, Mix joined the Sells-Floto Circus as its star attraction, drawing a salary of $10,000 a week. His show featured a portrayal of how

mail was carried in the days of the Pony Express, a presentation of expert ropers, trained horses, horsemanship, bronc busting, hard riding, and a great deal of showmanship, not unlike that of Buffalo Bill two decades earlier.

In 1932, while considering an offer from Universal Pictures to make sound films, Mix injured his leg in a riding accident. Newspaper accounts exaggerated his injury to such an extent that some stories claimed he was near death. This publicity brought thousands of letters from across the country pouring into Hollywood—the kids of America wanted Tom Mix back. Mix was reluctant until Will Hayes, the man who negotiated his contract at Universal, convinced him that America, in the midst of the Great Depression, would be encouraged by the news of a comeback by a man like Tom Mix. His first film for Universal, and his first talkie, was *Destry Rides Again,* an excellent story based on a popular book by Max Brand. The film was well received,

Tom Mix in the Fighting Cowboy, Tom Mix and Tony Jr. in Terror Trail, *and* Tom Mix and His Circus on the Barbary Coast, *Big Little and Better Little Books, Whitman, 1930s. Ted Hake collection.*

Framed photograph of Tom Mix and Tony. Ralston Purina Company sendaway radio premium for Tom Mix radio show Straight Shooters, *c. 1933. Ted Hake collection. (T.H.)*

but Mix was skeptical, quipping, "Hell, I don't know who's doing the talking, me or the horse." Some critics claimed his speech was unconvincing, but he went on to make eight more pictures. The box-office results were far from satisfying, and in 1933 Tom Mix retired from pictures. He did make a fifteen-chapter serial called *The Miracle Rider* in 1935, but he was tired and did not feel he could compete with the new singing cowboys—the new idols of kids who had grown up with radio and phonograph records.

The year he made *The Miracle Rider*, which put him back on matinee screens for fifteen weeks, Mix bought the giant Sam B. Dill Circus for $400,000. He renamed it the Tom Mix Circus and directed the show himself, modeling it after Buffalo Bill's Wild West Show. During his first tour with the circus, during the summer of 1935, Will Rogers died in a plane crash. Mix and Rogers had maintained their friendship from the days of Zack Mulhall's Wild West Show, and Mix was grieved and depressed. Two years later, because of severe competition, mounting costs, and the ongoing depression, the Tom Mix Circus folded.

On October 12, 1940, the man who had been called the Beau Brummell of the Wild West was wearing his sweeping ten-gallon

Tom Mix wooden gun. Ralston Company sendaway radio premium, 1934. Ted Hake collection. (T.H.)

Ralston Wheat Cereal package sample, c. 1933.

Stetson, cream-colored cowboy suit, the coat lined and corded with scarlet, patent leather boots stitched in red, white, and blue, and his diamond-studded platinum belt buckle with the famous brand that marked everything from his underwear to his horses—a big "M" with the first bar crossed to make a "T." He was driving his big custom-built Cord roadster with the longhorns mounted on the radiator, up from Tucson on his way to Phoenix. A bend in the road revealed a road crew working out a detour. He swerved to miss them, careened into a gully, and overturned. A metal suitcase came crashing onto his head, breaking his neck and killing him instantaneously.

The Ralston Tom Mix Radio Show—the most popular cowboy program of the airwaves—opened with organ music and hoofbeats, then the whinny of a horse, followed by "Up Tony, c'mon boy!" Then came a merry song describing Tom's favorite breakfast food:

> Shredded Ralston for your breakfast
> Starts the day off shining bright.
> Gives you lots of cowboy energy
> With a flavor that's just right.
> It's delicious and nutritious,
> Bite size and ready to eat.
> Take a tip from Tom,
> Go and tell your Mom—
> Shredded Ralston can't be beat!

After this commercial jingle that had millions of kids eating Shredded Ralston, an announcer said, "The Tom Mix Ralston Straight Shooters bring you action, mystery, and mile-a-minute thrills in radio's biggest Western detective program. Tonight you're about to hear another episode in a baffling mystery . . ."

During a commercial interlude, kids growing up in the era of the Great Depression or World War II would eagerly listen for the latest information on Tom Mix send-away premiums: "Boys! Girls! I'll send you my Horseshoe Nail Ring *Free!* For two Ralston box tops or one Ralston box top and ten cents in coin."

Tom Mix ring, Ralston send-away radio premium, 1935. Ted Hake collection. (T.H.)

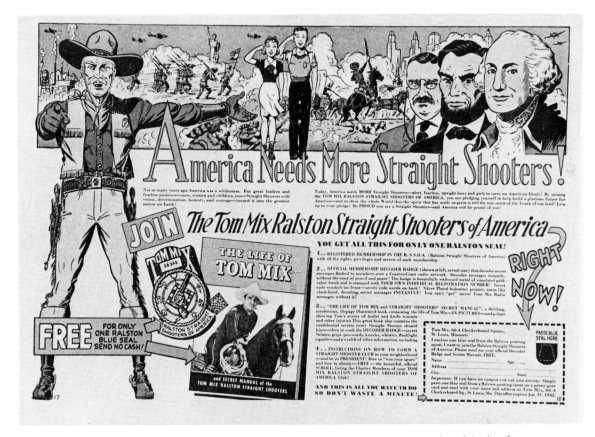

1942 newspaper comic-sheet advertisement offering membership in the Tom Mix Ralston Straight Shooters of America, an official membership decoder badge, and The Life of Tom Mix *secret manual. Ralston.*

American youngsters of the Depression yearned to explore the mythic cowboy folklore, the mysteries and adventures of the Wild West; and the Tom Mix radio show offered them a magical auditory world they could enter into with their own fantasy and imagination. Kids who played at Cowboys and Indians looked up to cowboy hero Tom Mix as a shining example of everything good that was fighting off the bad men of the world. Tuning in to Tom often brought a sense of true West color and adventure to what might otherwise have seemed a drab, humdrum, everyday world, and receiving a secret ring, badge, or whistle from Tom Mix in the mail gave boys and girls a sense of belonging to a Wild West world that was far, far away.

Perhaps it was only a sound man hitting coconut shells against a soundboard to create the hoofbeats of Tony the Wonder Horse, or just the crumpling of cellophane near a microphone to make the sound of a brush or barn fire, but to children sitting next to their family console in living rooms all over America in the thirties and forties, it was real enough. Mother was also indebted to Tom Mix, since Dick and Jane would now eat their breakfast cereal (as long as it was Ralston) without prodding.

Tom Mix began endorsing Ralston cereal products in 1933, the same year *The Ralston Tom Mix Radio Show* went on the air as a fifteen-minute NBC Blue (and later Mutual) network serial, eventually becoming a half-hour show. The show, sponsored from 1933 to 1950 by the Ralston Purina Company, was always the best written and performed afternoon serial and had more teenage and adult listeners than any other kids' show. Tom Mix himself never appeared on the show. It remained on the air ten years after his death, and his image appeared on the Ralston cereal box for several years after the show itself went off the air. The actors who impersonated Tom included Artells Dickson, Russell Thorson, Jack Holden, and Curley Bradley. The theme song was sung to the tune of "When It's Roundup Time in Texas" and "The Bloom Is on the Sage." Radio's Tom Mix lived on the "T-M Bar Ranch" in "Dobie Township." Tom's friends and cohorts were "Straight Shooters," and the moral of the program was that "Straight Shooters always win." Tony the Wonder Horse was

Cardboard sign offering regular, instant hot, or shredded Ralston cereal. Sendaway pinback buttons are from the Tom Mix radio show. Ted Hake collection.

always helping to rescue Tom from the bad guys. Other characters were the Old Wrangler, who would spout such homilies as, "Well, I'll be a lop-eared kangaroo with big black eyes, if it isn't round-up time!" and Sheriff Mike Shaw, Lee Loo the Chinese cook, Pecos Williams, Jimmy and Jane, and the man who repossessed the T-M Bar Ranch, Amos Q. Snood, the Scrooge of Dobie, known for his "Pink Pills for Pale People."

TOM MIX COLLECTIBLES

The radio show featured more secrets than the CIA: secret grips, signals, whistles, passwords, knocks, and salutes.

THE SECRET PASSWORD

"The secret password of the Straight Shooters is always given with the secret grip. It should never be spoken above a whisper. The password is given whenever a Straight Shooter wants to find out if another person is a member. The first Straight Shooter whispers the word 'RAL.' The second Straight Shooter should then whisper the word 'STON.' Afterwards, both Straight Shooters whisper 'RALSTON.' The password must be given at all secret meetings of the Straight Shooters."

A collection of Tom Mix Straight Shooter radio premiums. Left to right: *Postal Telegraph "International System" Signal Set, 1938; Tom Mix Western Movie; Rocket Parachute; signed photograph in aluminum frame with wooden base; periscope; telegraph set, 1940. Foreground: leather spurs, belt with buckle, Zyp Gun (1934) in front, telescope (1938) just behind spurs. Far right: Golden Plastic Bullet Telescope with Magic-Tone Bird-call (1950).*

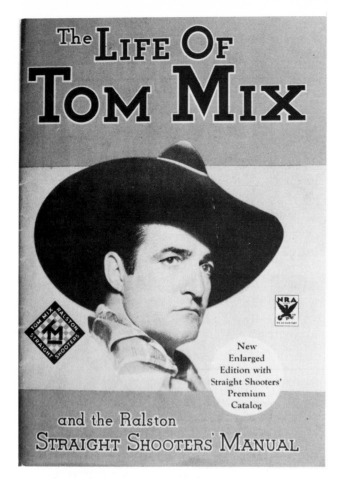

Above: The Life of Tom Mix *and the* Ralston Straight Shooters' Manual, *1934. Ted Hake collection.* Below: Tom Mix Secret Manual, *1944. Ted Hake collection.*

The show also offered scores of premiums. For a box top and a dime (or two box tops and no money) sent to Checkerboard Square, St. Louis, Missouri, you could get a

Tom Mix bandanna
western lariat
genuine leather cuffs
spurs with leather TM strap
paperboard face mask of Tom
zip gun in a TM envelope
Straight Shooter ring
lucky charm
branding iron
wooden gun in a holster and a cartridge belt
automatic pencil
Straight Shooter stationery
Western Movie (a cardboard box with a thirty-frame paper movie)
Straight Shooter's bracelet
cowboy chaps
The Trail of the Terrible Six
leather strap Lucky Wrist Band
sun watch
girl's dangle bracelet with four charms (the TM brand, Tom on Tony, a steer head, and a six-gun)
championship belt (in a red and black checkerboard pattern)
buckle
care instructions for live baby turtle (the turtle was branded)
movie makeup kit
telescope
wrangler's badge
ranch boss badge
famous Mystery Ring (look-in picture ring)
periscope
Indian blow gun and target
elephant-hair ring with instructions

The ID bracelet was described in a premium catalogue: "Both boys and girls will like this nifty silver-flashed identification bracelet. The checkerboard design band

Tom Mix Straight Shooter
Wrangler Badge,
Ralston Purina, 1934.
Ted Hake collection. (T.H.)

will remind you of the red-and-white box of scrumptious Hot Ralston every time you look at it. Yessirree! It has your very own initial on it and your own number listed in Tom Mix's Identification Bureau. So if you ever get lost and can't remember your name, just go to the nearest policeman and ask him to find out from the Tom Mix Ralston Straight Shooters. BONUS: With your bracelet, you will also receive a genuine fingerprint file card. Put your own fingerprints, name, and address on it and this card will be sent right to J. Edgar Hoover's F.B.I. offices in our nation's capital. It's official! Isn't that swell?"

During and after the war, plastics came of age and the premiums were cheaper and more intriguing. The most popular plastic used in premiums was the kind that stored up energy in the light and glowed in the dark. Some of these included a glow-in-the-dark ribbon and medal, glow-in-the-dark compass and magnifier, glow-in-the-dark spurs (aluminum with glow rowels), a Lucite signal arrowhead, a Magic-Light Tiger-Eye Ring, and a Golden Plastic Bullet Telescope with Magic Tone Birdcall.

The very first Tom Mix radio premium was the Horseshoe Nail Ring. This was a horseshoe nail that Ralston Straight Shooters had to bend into a ring with pliers. It was accompanied by a Straight Shooter manual, which told the glorified history of Tom Mix from Teddy Roosevelt Rough Rider to Texas Ranger to rodeo champion to movie star. One of the Straight Shooter manuals had the Tom Mix Chart of Wounds, showing Tom's twelve bullet wounds and forty-seven bone fractures. Not shown were his twenty-two knife wounds and the 4″ hole in his back caused by a dynamite explosion.

The rarest and most sought-after Tom Mix Ralston box-top premiums:
— The Compass–Magnifying Glass, made of silverlike nickel with a tiny compass and a magnifying glass that could be folded back. Offered originally in 1937, it has the single word JAPAN marked on the back.
— Two years later the show offered a brass Compass–Magnifying Glass decorated with western designs with the TM-Bar brand and the words "Ralston Straight Shooter" on the back.
— After the war a plastic Compass–Magnifying Glass was available. This was in the form of an arrowhead with the TM-Bar brand in rope script.
— The Compass-Gun was a 1½″ replica of a six-shooter. Made of glowing plastic, the gun had a metal barrel that was a magnet that pointed north when swinging from its chain. The chain was attached to a glow-plastic arrowhead that was a whistle. This could be a key chain for boys or a bracelet for girls. It had no TM-Bar identification.
— The Lucite Signal Arrowhead was 4½″ long. It had a magnifying lens, a reduction lens (called a "smallifying" glass), a set of musical pipes, and a spinning whistle siren.

Above: Tom Mix Comics Book #3, *Ralston Straight Shooters, 1941. Ted Hake collection. (T.H.)* Below: *Tom Mix Western comic published by Fawcett, 1949.*

—The wooden six-shooter was offered from 1933 until 1942. It was as large as a real gun, looked authentic, and had a barrel that broke and a cartridge drum that spun.

—The Decoder Badge had a dial indicator that was a movable six-shooter; it pointed to symbols like a horseshoe, a skull, or a star, which stood for messages like "danger ahead," "enemy," or "keep going."

Rings were the most popular of the radio premiums, and Tom Mix offered many different types to Ralston Straight Shooters. The basic ring had the Tom Mix brand against the Ralston checkerboard trademark. Later you could have your own initials on the top. After the war there was a Siren Ring with a block magnet on top, a Slide-Whistle ring, and the Tiger-Eye Ring that glowed in the dark. The most desirable and hardest to find is the Mystery Ring. The TM-Bar brand is on the top of the simulated gold band that holds a little box with a hole. Inside the hole is a photograph of Tom Mix and Tony magnified "100 times" and signed "To My Straight Shooter Pal, Tom Mix."

To complete your collection of Tom Mix premiums you would also have to have the Tom Mix spurs, made of solid metal with the TM-Bar brand stamped on the sides and glow-in-the-dark plastic rowels; the Bullet Telescope, 4″ long with a bird-call device; a toy television set (one of the last premiums offered) with a viewer for films showing photographs of the radio cast, Tom Mix mysteries in comic-strip form, and other pictures. This premium was a prelude to television, where Tom Mix movies were beginning to air.

The official publication of the Tom Mix Ralston Straight Shooters was *Tom Mix Comics*. *Tom Mix Comics* #1 and #2 were issued in 1940, issues #3 through #7 in

1941 and issues #8 and #9 in 1942. In 1942, issues #10, #11, and #12 became *Tom Mix Commandos Comics* and placed the cowboy star in a modern World War II setting with the Invisible Invaders featuring the Secrets of the Commandos and other sensational war stories.

Fawcett published *Tom Mix Western Comics* from 1948 through 1953 for a total of sixty-one issues. Of course, comics were a stepchild of the Big Little Books, those small-size books that were half novel, half picture, issued by Whitman, Saalfield, and other companies throughout the 1930s. Tom Mix was a favorite, and the series included:

Tom Mix, Riding Avenger
Tom Mix and His Circus on the Barbary Coast
Tom Mix and the Hoarde of Montezuma (The original illustrations for this book were done by Henry Vallely, and are considered exceptionally fine.)

Tom Mix and the Stranger from the South
Tom Mix and Tony, Jr., in Terror Trail
Tom Mix in The Fighting Cowboy
Tom Mix in The Range War
Tom Mix Plays a Lone Hand
Tom Mix, Chief of the Rangers
Tom Mix Rides to the Rescue
Tom Mix and the Riders of Death Valley
Tom Mix and the Texas Bad Man
Tom Mix in Tom Mason on Top

All of these were published by Whitman Publishing Company except for the last, *Tom Mix in Tom Mason on Top*, which was a Saalfield book. A Big Big Book, *Tom Mix and the Scourge of Paradise Valley*, was published in 1937, also with illustrations by Vallely. In 1939 *Tom Mix Avenges the Dry Gulched Range King* was published as a Fast Action Story. This is quite rare.

Tom Mix Avenges the Dry Gulched Range King, *a Fast-Action Story published in 1939;* Tom Mason on Top, starring Tom Mix, *published by Saalfield, 1935; tin-litho Japanese clicker toy after Tom Mix, c. 1950. (P.C.)*

Top left: *Tom Mix wristwatch, Ingersoll, 1934. Robert Lesser collection.* Above: *Tom Mix pocket watch, Ingersoll, 1933. The belt attachment contains real gold ore. Robert Lesser collection.* Left: *Linen bandanna, "Best wishes, Tom Mix," c. 1933. Ted Hake collection.*

The Life of Tom Mix manual, issued in 1933, and the premium catalogues and photos issued throughout the 1930s and '40s are excellent collectibles. Other books include *The Trail of the Terrible Six, The Mystery of the Flaming Warrior,* by George Lowther, published in 1947, and the 1934 illustrated hardcover book, *Tony and His Pal.* Tom Mix Circus posters are excellent graphic collectibles, and extremely rare. Movie collectibles include stills, publicity photos, lobby cards, one-sheet posters, and postcards. The postcards were also available in penny slot machines in amusement parks. Known to exist, but rare, are a Tom Mix and Tony child's

wooden horse on wheels and a 125-piece full-color jigsaw puzzle put out by Rexall Drug Stores. The top of the line in Tom Mix collectibles is the 1933 Ingersoll pocket watch. It features Tom astride a rearing Tony on the front and the slogan "Always Find Time for a Good Deed, Tom Mix" embossed on the back.

The Tom Mix Museum in Dewey, Oklahoma, is operated by the Oklahoma Historical Society. Some of its great treasures include Tom's $15,000 saddle, of sterling silver and hand-tooled black leather; Tom's clothes, guns, and riding gear; and a full-size replica of Tony, the world-renowned Wonder Horse.

Tom Mix and the Mystery of the Flaming Warrior, *by George Lowther, McMullen, 1947. (P.C.)*

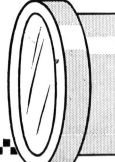

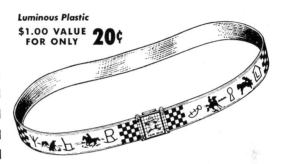

Giveaway flyer for Tom Mix premiums, 1949. Robert Lesser collection.

Lone Ranger painted plaster doll, 15" high, amusement park and carnival prize, c. 1945.

THE LONE RANGER

By 1930 there were 26 million radio sets in homes across America; 85 percent of the population was "tuned in." The Wall Street stock-market crash of October 1929 had initiated a long gray decade characterized by both despair and a promise of progress and better times to come. Many who could not afford to go to the picture show at the Ritz or Rialto found their contentment in sitting around the big RCA Victor console radio and listening to an exciting audio world of dance band music and comedy, variety, and dramatic shows. For boys and girls of the Depression, tales of fantasy adventure usually came over the airwaves just after 4:30 P.M., when they rushed home from school to listen in to *Jack Armstrong, the All-American Boy, Dick Tracy, Junior G-Men, Bobby Benson's Adventures, Buck Rogers in the 25th Century, Flash Gordon, Mark Trail, Tom Mix,* and *Little Orphan Annie.* All of these radio shows offered premiums, send-away prizes, and gifts to youngsters who were sometimes feeling desolate and deprived in a land where pennies were said to fall from the sky when it rained—at least that's what the happy songs were telling (or selling) everybody.

The 1930s were a time of innocence in America, a time of three-little-pigs-cheer commingled with the fury and menace of the Big Bad Wolf. A Silly Symphony rodent imp named Mickey Mouse, with black balloon ears, red pants, and clown shoes, brought a sense of relief through cartoon fun into the weary hearts of millions, as did Shirley Temple, a tap-dancing sweetheart with golden corkscrew curls and a matching sunny-side-up disposition. Dick Powell, Ruby Keeler, Joan Blondell, Ginger Rogers, and a chorus of sarcastic hard-boiled gum-chewing Busby Berkeley dames with platinum hair, black-mascara eyes, and raspberry-red lips certainly could take those on the dole out of their doldrums. But for a bunch of kids tuned in to radio station WXYZ in and around Detroit, Michigan, on January 30, 1933—in the worst year of the Depression—there was a new escape; the great cowboy hero avenger of American morality was first heard crying out, "Hi Yo Silver! A–W–A–AY!" The fictitious mysterious Masked Man of the Wild West, the Lone Ranger, was soon to become one of the most popular radio characters, cowboy or otherwise, to emerge out of the Depression, his trail-blazing gallop of righteousness continuing into the decades that followed. A man of law and order, an idealist who acted on his beliefs, was needed at this time to inspire confidence and zeal in American youngsters. The Lone Ranger and his sidekick Indian pal, Tonto, filled this bill on the radio and later in films and on television. If America was to remain safe for democracy, it depended on popular-culture characters of powerful virtue like the Lone Ranger to show the way.

The actual Texas Rangers were originally appointed without pay by the Spanish government in the early 1800s to protect settlers against Indian attack. In 1874, after the disruption of the Civil War, this Texas Ranger force was reorganized into two battalions, one to work in Indian country in the West, the other to handle border violations along the Rio Grande, and mainly to suppress cattle rustling by bands of cowboy outlaws. Although the force went through many up and down periods, it still exists today, the Texas Rangers remaining a symbol of the taming of the old Wild West frontier. Masked riders did exist in the Old West; they were usually Mexican banditos who wore a black half-face mask as they robbed and killed. But it was the mythic character of old California—Zorro, the Masked Avenger, created by novelist John-

"Hi-Yo Silver," Lone Ranger rayon tie, The Lone Ranger, Inc., c. 1939.

ston McCulley and played in silent movies by Douglas Fairbanks, Sr.—who influenced the concept of the Lone Ranger. Republic Pictures produced a series of Zorro twelve-chapter serials in the 1930s, including *Zorro Rides Again,* with John Carroll, *Zorro's Black Whip, Son of Zorro, Ghost of Zorro,* and *Zorro's Fighting Legion,* with Reed Hadley.

The original radio account of the Lone Ranger was centered on a fictionalized story about six Texas Rangers led by a Captain Dan Reid who was determined to stop the Cavendish Gang, a band of vicious outlaws who attacked ranches and wagon trains, robbing and killing their victims. Butch Cavendish, the leader of the gang, had enlisted a man named Collins, whom Dan Reid trusted to take the Rangers to what was supposed to be the secret hiding place of the gang; but instead it was a trap. An ambush by the Cavendish Gang at Bryant's Gap left all but one of the six Texas

Zorro blue plastic drinking cup, 1950s. Courtesy of A Touch of Us.

Rangers dead. The sole survivor—who appeared to have been killed but still had life in his injured body—was John Reid, the captain's younger brother. A clever Indian, discovering the bodies, saw the one that was close to death. The Indian dug six graves, burying the five corpses and giving one of the graves the appearance of containing the sixth victim. Then he carried John Reid back to his camp, where he nursed his wounds and, after four days, brought him back to consciousness. The two men realized as they talked that they had been boyhood friends and that John had saved the Indian from death when they were both children growing up on the western plains. Tonto told the wounded Ranger, whom he called "Kemo-Sabe," meaning faithful friend, what he had discovered at Bryant's Gap, pronouncing, "You . . . lone Ranger!" Choosing to remain dead in the eyes of the Cavendish Gang, John Reid vehemently declared, "I am the Lone Ranger!"

He decided that it was to be his mission to avenge his brother's death by bringing the Cavendish Gang and all other outlaws and crooks in the West to justice. Wearing a black Zorro-like face mask to conceal his identity, the Lone Ranger became a mystery man of the frontier who dedicated his life to the service of humanity and country.

Out on the plains John Reid, now the Lone Ranger, came upon a fiery white stallion engaged in a fierce, to-the-death battle with a raging buffalo. When the Lone Ranger saw that the mad buffalo was about to kill the beautiful white horse, he fired two silver bullets into the immense black animal, which fell dead on the spot. Tonto and the Lone Ranger brought the badly wounded horse back to health, whereupon the Lone Ranger decided he should be set free. However, the wild white horse, now calm and grateful, chose to stay with his rescuer—and was given the name "Silver."

The Lone Ranger had once promised that if anything befell his brother, he would find Dan's wife and son and give them their rightful share of the brothers' silver mine. This secret mine was the source of the Lone Ranger's famous silver bullets. Even though he had received information that his brother's wife and baby boy had been killed in an Indian massacre, he continued to search for them until he could find conclusive evidence.

One day, after thirteen years of western law-and-justice adventures, the Lone Ranger stopped at a ranch where he found a dying old woman named Grandma Frisbee and a teenaged boy with the name of Dan. As the old lady lay dying, she told a story she had kept secret from the boy, revealing that he was not her grandson at all. Recounting a harrowing tale of an Indian massacre years earlier, Grandma Frisbee said she had been the only survivor, and had somehow managed to escape with a baby boy. She showed the Lone Ranger a gold locket she had kept, given to her by the boy's mother just before she was killed in the attack, containing a picture of her husband, the baby's father. The Masked Man, realizing the boy standing before him was his long-lost nephew, told them that he, the Lone Ranger, was the brother of Dan Reid. The old lady, overjoyed, asked to have a look at the masked rider's face before she expired, and proclaimed, "It's a good face!" Ecstatic to find that this heroic, mysterious man was his uncle and to learn of his true identity, young Dan listened as his newfound role model told him about the heritage left him by his own father and the good woman who had brought him up. "Yes, yours is a great heritage," the Lone Ranger said over the airwaves in deep baritone masculine tones. "They and others like them have handed down to you the right to worship as you choose, and the right to work and profit from your enter-

Lone Ranger doll, 1938. Robert Lesser collection. (P.C.) Tonto doll, 1938. Robert Lesser collection. (P.C.)

Comic book: The Lone Ranger's Famous Horse Hi-Yo Silver, Dell Publishing Co., 1957. (P.C.) Comic book: The Lone Ranger, Dell, 1950. (P.C.)

prise. They have given you a land where there is true freedom, true equality of opportunity, a nation that is governed by the people by laws that are best for the greatest number. Your duty, Dan, is to preserve that heritage, and strengthen it. That is the heritage and duty of every American."

This radio cowboy hero, expressing and living out a credo of American patriotism based on law, truth, justice, and bold action, offered a sense of hope for people in a fear-ridden Depression who needed to continue to believe in the American Dream. The Lone Ranger became an American institution, as much a folk hero as any of the real cowboy heroes of the early West.

The Lone Ranger was first conceived of by George W. Trendle, a pioneering tycoon who had turned a single nickelodeon into a chain of motion picture theaters in Detroit. Eventually the theaters were sold to Paramount, but Trendle remained as the head of United Detroit Theaters. His cowboy radio hero had to be a man of mystery, he thought, perhaps one with a secret identity. Together with Fran Striker, a writer from Buffalo, New York, whom Trendle hired to write the first trial script, the concept was developed of a lone individual fighting for justice. Trendle wanted his character to embody answered prayers, to be accepting and kindly toward all racial and religious groups; he demanded of Striker, the writer, that he use "good grammar" whenever the hero spoke. After a good many rewrites and countless revisions on their initial script, Striker and Trendle came up with twelve scripts featuring the Lone Ranger, Tonto, and the mighty white horse, Silver. The first was put on the air over WXYZ-Detroit with little advance promotion on January 30, 1933. The two men decided it would be a good idea to test the effect of their show by offering free souvenir programs to the first 300 children who wrote in to the station. When 25,000 letters came in, Trendle and Striker knew they had a winner. In July of that year they sent out an announcement that the Lone Ranger would make a personal appearance at a high-school football field, and 70,000 hysterical fans showed up, screaming for their new cowboy hero.

Initially the show's creators avoided using premiums, feeling that this would detract from the Lone Ranger's image of idealism, perfectionism, and patriotism. This posture had shifted by 1935, when Silver-

cup Bread issued the first Lone Ranger Safety Scout Membership Badge. By 1938 a major merchandising blitz swept the country in department stores, five-and-tens, newsstands, and supermarkets and over the airwaves. The Lone Ranger character was also licensed to appear on watches, food products, games, toys, belts and other clothing articles, to the delight of youngsters across America, most of whom loved to play at Cowboys and Indians, Good Guys and Bad Guys.

America in the 1930s, led by J. Edgar

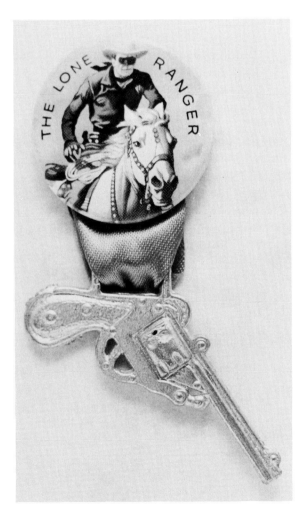

Litho-on-metal pin with small white metal gun, 1950s. Courtesy Peanut Butter & Jane.

Sendaway radio premium photo of the Lone Ranger, TLR Inc., 1939.

Lone Ranger radio premium ring with sliding top secret compartment, issued during World War II and decorated with military insignia. Ted Hake collection. (T.H.)

Hoover and his fastidious FBI, became obsessed with the idea of sustaining morality in the midst of chaos. There were leftist groups, angry strikers, breadlines, men on relief, and criminals who were regarded as Robin Hoods. John Dillinger, Clyde Barrow with his sweetheart Bonnie Parker, Pretty Boy Floyd, and others were compared to the desperadoes of the Old West, holding up banks with wild gun-shooting chases across the western and midwestern states. Youngsters joined Junior G-Men Clubs under the guidance of real life G-Man hero Melvin Purvis, who eventually shot and killed Public Enemy Number One Dillinger at the Biograph Movie Theatre in Chicago. The Lone Ranger was deliberately patterned after this kind of aggressive G-Man–FBI patriotism that sought to wipe out crooks from the land; and American kids growing up during the Depression, World War II, and the 1950s Eisenhower years took the Lone Ranger credo and ethics to heart. Receiving a membership badge, Ranger's gun, secret manual, or ring in the mail from the Lone Ranger meant belonging to that segment of America that was fighting a war against crime or against other enemies across the oceans.

Above: *Lone Ranger Official Cowboy Outfit: gun, holster, original box, 1938. Ted Hake collection.* Right: *Lone Ranger wristwatch in original box, 1939. Robert Lesser collection.*

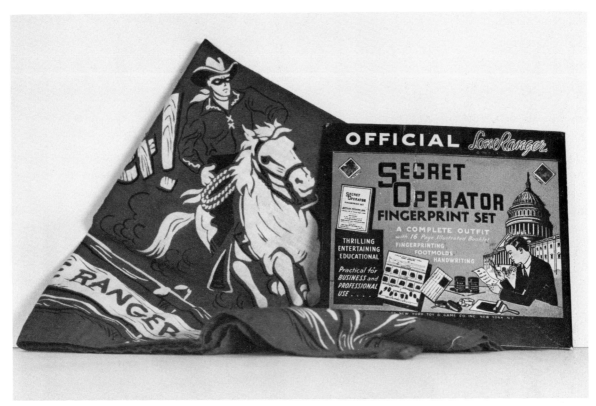

Above: *Linen neckerchief and official Lone Ranger Secret Operator Set, 1939.*
Ted Hake collection. (T.H.) Below: *Lone Ranger Blackout Kit: "It glows in the*
dark," 1942. Ted Hake collection. (T.H.)

The original opening of the Lone Ranger radio show went as follows:

Theme: "William Tell Overture," by Rossini.

Bridge Music: "Les Preludes," by Liszt.

Opening: Theme up full and under . . . Hoofbeats fade in . . .

RANGER: Hi-yo Silver!!! *(Gunshots and hoofbeats.)*

ANNOUNCER: A fiery horse with the speed of light, a cloud of dust and a hearty hi-yo Silver! The Lone Ranger! *(Theme up full and under.)* With his faithful Indian companion, Tonto, the daring and resourceful Masked Rider of the plains led the fight for law and order in the early western United States. Nowhere in the pages of history can one find a greater champion of justice. Return with us now to those thrilling days of yesteryear . . . *(Hoofbeats fade in.)* From out of the past come the thundering hoofbeats of the great horse Silver. The Lone Ranger rides again!!!

RANGER: Come on, Silver! Let's go, big fellow! Hi-yo Silver! Away!! *(Theme up full.)*

The trumpeting chords of Rossini's "William Tell Overture" became forever identified to kids of the 1930s, '40s, and '50s as the Lone Ranger music. During a performance by the Detroit Symphony Orchestra in 1937, a young Lone Ranger fan, recognizing the chords that serve as the masked horseman's theme, leaped up and yelled, "Hi-yo Silver! Away!"

When spoken, the name "the Lone Ranger" was always uttered in a tone of wonderment and unabashed awe. Often a bystander or a central character in the radio series would ask—as the Lone Ranger galloped off with Tonto toward the distances beyond and new adventures to come—"Who was that masked man?" The reply being, "Why, don't you know? That man was . . . the Lone Ranger!"

The two actors most closely associated with the deep baritone voice of the Lone Ranger on the radio were Earle Graser and Brace Beemer. Beemer had been the Masked Man in the 1930s for just a few months when Graser took over, but when Graser was killed in a car crash in 1941, Beemer returned to the role, remaining in it until the last live broadcast on September 3, 1954. John Todd, a former Shakespearean actor, played the part of the stolid, monosyllabic Tonto during the show's entire run on the air. Well-known actors who at one time or another played on a *Lone Ranger* radio episode included Danny Thomas and John Hodiak.

Fran Striker continued throughout as the chief writer and story editor. He also wrote a popular series of Lone Ranger novels, which was published by Grosset & Dunlap.

The Masked Man appeared in film in the successful movie serial *The Lone Ranger,* with fifteen chapters, produced by Republic Pictures in 1938. Kids loved to see Lee Powell portraying the Lone Ranger radio hero on the screen with a real Indian actor named Chief Thundercloud playing Tonto. *The Lone Ranger Rides Again* was the second serial, again with fifteen chapters, produced in 1939. In this movie serial Bob Livingston played the Ranger, with Chief Thundercloud repeating as Tonto.

The Lone Ranger premiered on television on September 15, 1949, starring Clayton Moore, an actor who had become known as the last "King of the Serials." Before donning the mask of the Lone Ranger, he had had starring roles in *Perils of Nyoka, Jesse James Rides Again, The Adventures of Frank and Jesse James, G-Men Never Forget,* and *Ghost of Zorro.* His background suited him for the role of

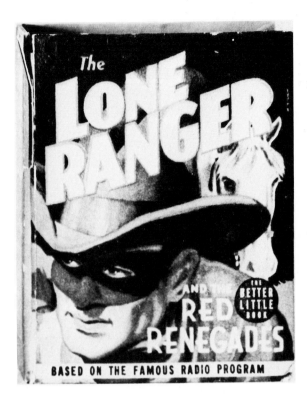

The Lone Ranger and the Red Renegades,
Better Little Book, Whitman. (P.C.)

The Lone Ranger, *by Fran Striker, illustrated hardcover book #1 with dust jacket,
Grosset & Dunlap, 1936.* The Lone Ranger
and the Black Shirt Highwayman, *Better
Little Book, Whitman, 1939.*

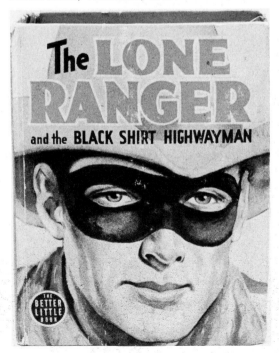

the Masked Man, and he was a first-rate
actor who could also handle his own riding
and stunts with flair and virility. Moore
and his sidekick, Jay Silverheels, remained
on the show until it ended in 1961 and
were greatly admired by the 5 million TV
viewers. They also appeared with Bonita
Granville in a color motion picture, *The
Lone Ranger,* distributed by Warner
Brothers in 1956, and in *The Lone Ranger
and the City of Gold,* a color film from
United Artists in 1958.

A Lone Ranger cartoon series was produced by CBS network TV in 1966, with an
estimated 3 million viewers in summer and
7 million in winter for the half-hour pro-
gramming slot. The Lone Ranger appeared
in many special circus and rodeo shows, always astride a silver-white horse and always wearing a mask. Sometimes other
famous characters, like Roy Rogers or the

Lone Ranger litho all-metal lunch box, TLR Inc., manufactured by Adco-Liberty Mfg. Corp., Newark, N.J., c. 1938.

The Official Lone Ranger First Aid Kit, manufactured by American White Cross Labs, for the Lone Ranger Safety Club members, 1938. (P.C.)

dog Lassie, would appear together with the Lone Ranger at Madison Square Garden or other events. The first official Lone Ranger appearance of this type was in the Olympia Circus at the Chicago Stadium in 1940.

In 1954 the Lone Ranger, Tonto, Silver, commercial tie-ins, radio scripts and shows, and TV episodes were all sold by George Trendle to Jack Wrather, a wealthy oilman industrialist, and his wife, Bonita Granville, for the then top sum of $3 million cash. Trendle, who had turned the Lone Ranger into a multimillion-dollar living legend, insisted that the Wrather Corporation of Beverly Hills maintain the high moral standards associated with the Lone Ranger character so painstakingly created by himself and Fran Striker.

In 1979 the Los Angeles Superior Court issued an injunction forbidding Clayton Moore from wearing "the Lone Ranger mask or any mask substantially similar in appearance." Moore still makes personal appearances as the Lone Ranger, but now wears black masklike dark glasses pending his appeal of the decision. Fans still recognize him as the Lone Ranger, and he and Brace Beemer, the first radio Ranger, will always be associated with that character in the public's mind.

The most recent feature film is *The Legend of the Lone Ranger* (1981), a Universal City and Jack Wrather production, beautifully filmed in color on actual location in Texas, starring Klinton Spilsbury as the Lone Ranger, Michael Horse as Tonto, and Jason Robards as President Ulysses S. Grant.

LONE RANGER COLLECTIBLES

A would-be cowboy could tell time by his Lone Ranger wristwatch, keep his pencils in a Lone Ranger pencil box, and do his penmanship exercises on a Lone Ranger writing tablet. He could color in a Lone Ranger coloring book, put together Lone

Lone Ranger school bag, vinyl and canvas, c. 1946. Courtesy of Topeo.

Lone Ranger and Tonto school bag, leatherette, c. 1940. Courtesy of Topeo.

Ranger jigsaw puzzles, paste up Lone Ranger cards in a Lone Ranger scrapbook, and on Halloween dress up as his Ranger hero himself, wearing a black mask and cowboy hat, with two Lone Ranger guns set in a Lone Ranger holster belt. An eager listener-member of the Lone Ranger Safety Club could wear his radio premium badges and silver-bullet rings, blow his Lone Ranger whistle, read his Lone Ranger National Defender's Secret Portfolio, use a Lone Ranger toothbrush, eat his cereal in a

Lone Ranger bowl, and drink his milk in a Hi-Yo Silver Tumbler. If he cut himself on a hiking expedition with the Boy Scouts, he could use a bandage from his special Lone Ranger safety kit. He could practice his marksmanship by firing a special gun at his Lone Ranger target game. There was no end to the mass-produced Lone Ranger merchandise, and these items are the Lone Ranger collectibles of today.

Between 1938 and 1941 the Masked Rider of the Plains was sponsored by a number

The Lone Ranger Rides Again, *one-sheet poster for the 15-chapter Republic serial, with Robert Livingston as the Lone Ranger and Chief Thunder-cloud as Tonto, 1939.*

of bread companies, including Bond Bread and Butter-Nut Bread. Silvercup Bread, the first regional sponsor, was not named, as many believed, after the famous horse Silver. This was a coincidence. Silvercup and the other bread companies promoted a Safety Club, which got the radio listeners to send away for the manuals, newsletters, membership badges, club cards, postcard photos, Secret Writing Manuals, Good Luck tokens, and Solid Silver bullets. Merita Bread sponsored the *Lone Ranger* radio show in the South and sent out a giveaway black cardboard mask.

Tonto's Map of South West Texas is an interesting bread company sendaway issued when Earl Graser, the actor who portrayed the Lone Ranger on the radio, died in an auto accident. As explained by Cactus Pete, this was an illustrated map de-

signed to find the Lone Ranger, who was missing. For nine weeks you were supposed to trace Tonto's hieroglyphics (until Brace Beemer took over the role). This map, produced by the Gordon Baking Company, is a beautiful graphic and a valuable and prized collectible today.

In 1941 General Mills took over sponsorship of the show nationwide, and they urged eager kiddies to eat Kix, Wheaties, and Cheerios in order to get the number of box tops they needed to send in for their premium rings and membership badges. During the war the premiums were National Defenders Secret Portfolio, National Defenders Warning Siren, a glow-in-the-dark safety belt, a .45-caliber secret compartment Silver Bullet with actual ore inside, a Texas cattleman's belt, Victory Corps taps and manuals, a Secret Compartment Ring

Le Justicier Masqué, *French one-sheet personally autographed poster, with Clayton Moore as the Lone Ranger and Jay Silverheels as Tonto, a Jack Wrather production with Bonita Granville, released through United Artists in 1958.*

Program from the Olympia Circus at the Chicago Stadium, one of the first public appearances of the Lone Ranger, 1939.

available with four different military insignia (with a sliding panel that revealed photos of the Lone Ranger and Silver underneath), a blackout kit, an Atom Bomb Ring, a Weather Ring, and a Flashlight Gun with a secret compartment handle.

A prized premium issued in 1948 was Frontier Town. You could send away for the buildings with Cheerios box tops, complete with instructions for assembling the different sections.

There was a flashlight ring to send away for, a six-shooter ring, a pedometer, a Silver Bullet with a compass and a secret compartment, a movie-film ring, a bandanna, a secret compartment "Deputy Badge," and a "Deputy" Secret Folder.

In the years 1951–56, before the radio show gave way to television, you could still get a filmstrip saddle ring, which had 16mm film with glow-in-the-dark surfaces, color contest postcards, life-size posters of the Lone Ranger and Tonto, a Wheaties Hike-O-Meter, Wheaties Mystery Backs (this was a mystery printed on the back of a Wheaties box that contained a secret clue

inside, so you had to buy it), and eight Wheaties masks. General Mills continued its sponsorship of the *Lone Ranger* on television and in the late 1950s relinquished a portion of its commercial time to Cracker Jacks and Popsicle.

The Lone Ranger has been seen as a syndicated newspaper comic strip in 250 daily newspapers and 53 foreign publications. Charles Flanders has been acknowledged as the best of the Lone Ranger comic-strip artists. The strips were reprinted by Dell Publishing Company from 1938 to 1947 in comic-book form. The first issues were in black and white, and they later became four-color. A new Dell series began in 1948 and continued through 1962. In this series issue #1 through #37 were also newspaper-strip reprints, but with issue #38 the Lone Ranger got a new outfit and new stories. Clayton Moore was featured on his first cover with issue #112. Silver had his own comics from 1952 to 1960. There was also a *Silver and Tonto* quarterly and an annual 98-page *Lone Ranger Treasury*. In 1939 two now-scarce collectible comic books

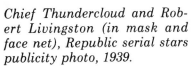
Chief Thundercloud and Robert Livingston (in mask and face net), Republic serial stars publicity photo, 1939.

were released: *Hi-Yo Silver—The Lone Ranger to the Rescue* and an ice-cream company giveaway with drawings by Henry Vallely. In 1954 there were two small Cheerios giveaway booklets entitled *The Lone Ranger and the Story of Silver* and *The Lone Ranger, His Mask and How He Met Tonto*. These are quite rare and hard to find.

Pressbooks, lobby cards, and one-sheet posters for the 1938 and 1939 serials, the 1956 Warner Brothers film, and the 1957 United Artists film are excellent Lone Ranger graphic collectibles. There was also a first-rate pulp series called *The Lone Ranger Magazine*, first issued in 1937.

A series of popular Lone Ranger novels by Fran Striker were published by Grosset & Dunlap, beginning in 1936 with *The Lone Ranger* and following with:

The Lone Ranger and the Mystery Ranch
The Lone Ranger and the Gold Robbery
The Lone Ranger and the Outlaw Stronghold
The Lone Ranger and Tonto
The Lone Ranger at the Haunted Gulch
The Lone Ranger Traps the Smuggler
The Lone Ranger Rides Again
The Lone Ranger Rides North
The Lone Ranger and the Silver Bullet
The Lone Ranger on the Powder Horn Trail
The Lone Ranger in Wild Horse Canyon
The Lone Ranger in West of Maverick Pass
The Lone Ranger on Gunsight Mesa
The Lone Ranger and the Bitter Spring Feud

This book series was published into the 1950s, and those with the original dust jackets intact are highly sought after by collectors of Western books as well as by Lone Ranger memorabilia collectors. Some of these were condensed into the popular Big Little Books or Better Little Book se-

ries (Whitman Publishers), which were made to fit into the pocket of a boy's mackinaw, or into his Lone Ranger metal lunch box with a tin litho of the Masked Man on it, or into a Lone Ranger school briefcase. Big Little Books were often a child's first introduction to the novel form, costing only 10 cents at Woolworth's or McCrory's Five and Dime. Big Little Book and Better Little Book titles include:

Lone Ranger and Dead Men's Mine
Lone Ranger and His Horse Silver
Lone Ranger and the Black Shirt Highwayman
Lone Ranger and the Great Western Span
Lone Ranger and the Menace of Murder Valley
Lone Ranger and the Red Renegades
Lone Ranger and the Secret Killer
Lone Ranger and the Secret of Somber Canyon
Lone Ranger and the Secret Weapon
Lone Ranger and the Silver Bullets
Lone Ranger and the Vanishing Herd
Lone Ranger Follows Through
Lone Ranger on the Barbary Coast
Lone Ranger and the Lost Valley
Lone Ranger Outwits Crazy Cougar

Whitman also issued a 94-page hardcover book in 1940 based on the radio show and in 1950 a Tall Better Little Book called *Secret of Somber Cavern*. In 1938 Grosset & Dunlap issued a 28-page hardcover book based on the Lone Ranger movie serial entitled *The Texas Renegades*. In 1951 Sandpiper issued a 78-page hardcover book with a dust jacket, entitled *The Lone Ranger's New Deputy*.

If you didn't have a radio or television, and you didn't eat Silvercup or Merita Bread or Kix or Wheaties or Cheerios, you could still collect Lone Ranger cowboy paraphernalia. It was available in every toy store, clothing store, department store, five-and-ten, and candy store in the land.

Counterclockwise from above: *Container for Lone Ranger "Silver Bullet" Pops, Candy Corporation of America, c. 1940. Robert Lesser collection. (P.C.) Lone Ranger Pops container. Robert Lesser collection. (P.C.) Matchbook "Lone Ranger Cones," TLR Inc., Maryland-Pacific Cone Co., late 1930s. Bond Bread store giveaway ink blotter, c. 1939.*

Lone Ranger Signal Siren Flashlight, litho on metal and plastic, Usalite, 1945. (P.C.)

There were:
  official cowboy outfits
  dolls
  soap in the shape of the Lone Ranger, Tonto, and Silver
  official belt sets
  school bags
  hand puppets
  record players
  tin pop-gun rifle
  Winchester Shooting "shell" rifle
  gun-holster suitcase
  sports kit, which included a football
  tin targets by Marx (made in three different sizes, with beautiful tin-litho graphics on all of them)
  official holster sets
  English cookie tin
  Lone Ranger games
  authentic punch-out set
  large and small metal cork guns
  soda tumblers
  mask and belt sets
  Tonto outfit
  pencil boxes
  puzzle sets
  large and small hairbrush
  printing sets
  carnival chalk figures
  crayons
  card games
  tattoos-picture book
  wallets
  toothbrush holders
  ring toss game
  Lone Ranger Strong Box
  mask and watch set
  telescope
  Lone Ranger boy's tie
  signal flashlight
  Press Action toy
  jail keys
  harmonica
  Lone Ranger and Tonto plastic figures made by Hartland
  transfer decals

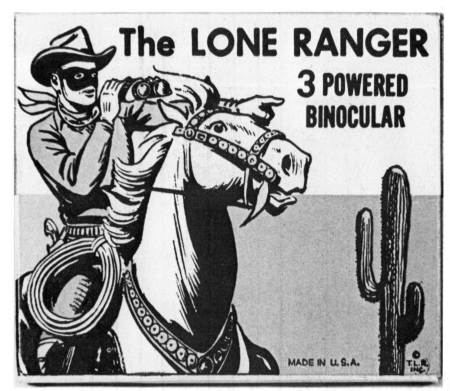

The Lone Ranger Binocular box, TLR Inc., 1940s.

Lone Ranger binoculars, plastic, 1940s.

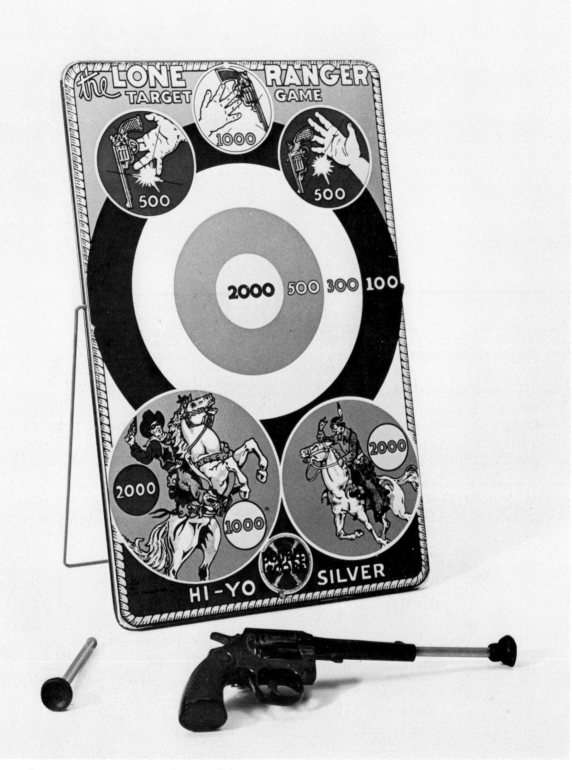

Lone Ranger target game, chromo-litho-graphed tin with stand, metal gun, and plunger darts, manufactured by Louis Marx Toy Company, 1938.

lithographed tin Marx wind-up Lone Ranger atop Silver (very desirable)

Marx Clicker pistol

Marx Sparkling gun

Marx also made a chuck-wagon lantern. Pennants, programs, buttons, matches, and other souvenir items issued in conjunction with personal appearances at circuses and rodeos are considered valuable collectibles. A very rare pinback Lone Ranger button sold at circuses shows a dark horse instead of a white one and a rider who does not wear a mask!

Gum Incorporated issued five 8″ x 10″ color cards made from sketches during the filming of the Lone Ranger serial in 1938. A smaller series of gum cards was issued in 1939. In 1940 Gum Incorporated issued a set of forty-eight full-color gum cards with action pictures of the Lone Ranger and Tonto. These cards could be obtained by saving twenty-five wrappers from Lone Ranger Bubble Gum, plus 10 cents.

No list of Lone Ranger Cowboy Collectibles can be complete without mentioning the wristwatch and pocket watch in the

Chuck Wagon Lantern with the original box, 1945. Ted Hake collection.

1939 Montgomery Ward mail-order catalogue. The New Haven Watch and Clock Company designed the first Lone Ranger wristwatch; it was distributed exclusively by the Everbrite Watch Company. The watch was made in small and large sizes for boys and girls. The Lone Ranger appears on the face of both the pocket watch and the wristwatch. If you can find the enameled watch fob to go with these, you are indeed lucky.

MORE RADIO THRILLS

Red Ryder

The exciting radio series *Red Ryder,* a Western adventure show based on the comic strip by Fred Harmon, first appeared on the Blue network in early 1942. Later the show was transferred to Mutual, where it was heard into the early 1950s. It opened with Little Beaver's catch phrase:

"You betchum, Red Ryder!" then music, hoofbeats, and an announcer crying out: "From out of the West comes America's famous fighting cowboy—Red Ryder!" The show's producer, writer, and director was Paul Franklin; Red Ryder was played at various times by Reed Hadley, Carlton Kadell, and Brooke Temple, and Little Beaver by Tommy Cook and Henry Blair. Radio premiums from this show are mostly from the 1942–45 period; they include a membership pin showing Red Ryder on his horse with the words "Victory Patrol," a paper sliding decoder, a paper rodeomatic decoder, a Red Ryder lucky coin with a hole in it, to wear on a chain, and a pony contest pin with a picture of Ryder on horseback and the words "I have entered the Red Ryder pony contest."

Red Ryder, drawn by Fred Harmon, appeared in comic sheets, comic books, coloring books, and hardback books. He had a long, square, handsome face and red hair

Two Better Little Books: Red Ryder and the Outlaw of Painted Valley, *1943;* Red Ryder the Fighting Westerner, *1940. Whitman. (P.C.)*

and wore a red shirt. Little Beaver was his small, impish Indian sidekick whose trousers were always falling down. Merchandise featuring Red Ryder and Little Beaver was created for department stores, toy stores, and five-and-tens, including games, clay sets, dart boards, outfits, and toys. On film Red Ryder was played by Republic's Don "Red" Barry in the early 1940s, and Bobby Blake, a child actor, took on the part of Little Beaver. Later "Wild Bill" Elliott became very successful as Red Ryder when he took over the film role from Don Barry.

Other desirable Red Ryder–Little Beaver paper collectibles are the comics published by Dell from September 1940 through April 1957. Issues #1 through #49 were newspaper-strip reprints and included *Alley Oop, Freckles and His Friends, Dan Dunn, Captain Easy,* and *The King of the Royal Mounted.* With issue #50 new Red Ryder stories appeared. The title was altered to *Red Ryder Ranch Magazine* with issue #145 and featured photos instead of drawings. In 1943 there was a Red Ryder Victory Patrol Superbook giveaway, and in 1950 Wells Lamont Corporation published another giveaway featuring the 1941 reprints. In 1941 Whitman published *Red Ryder and the Secret of Wolf Canyon* and *Red Ryder and the Mystery of Whispering Walls,* both in hardcover with dust jackets. *The Thunder Trail* was published in 1956. Whitman's Better Little Books (or Tall Better Little Books) are:

Red Ryder, Acting Sheriff
Red Ryder and Circus Luck
Red Ryder and Little Beaver on Hoofs of Thunder
Red Ryder and the Code of the West
Red Ryder and the Outlaw of Painted Valley
Red Ryder and the Rimrock Killer
Red Ryder and the Secret Canyon
Red Ryder and the Squaw-Tooth Rustlers

The Red Ryder Daisy Air Rifles, advertisement from The Open Road for Boys, December 1940. Red Ryder and Little Beaver Paint Book, Whitman, 1947.

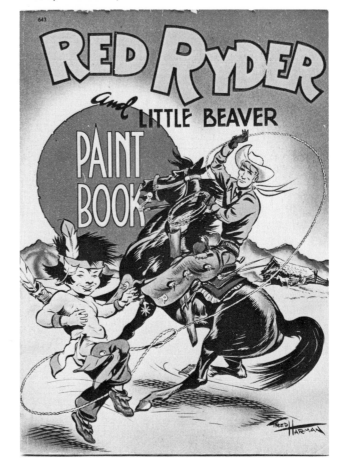

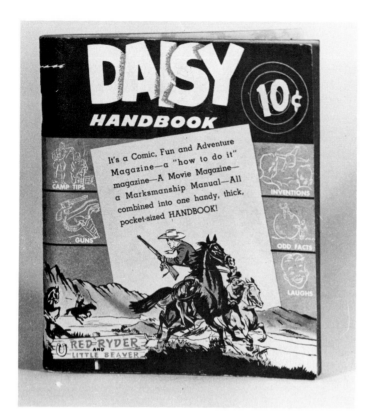

A Daisy Handbook, *published in 1946 by Daisy Manufacturing Company, featuring Fred Harman's Red Ryder and Little Beaver, Buck Rogers comics, tips on branding and saddling horses, cowboy talk, and valuable premium offers for the Red Ryder Cowboy Carbine 1000-shot repeater rifle. (P.C.)*

Red Ryder wristwatch, a rare cowboy collectible, 1949. Robert Lesser collection. Red Ryder canvas and leatherette gloves, c. 1946. Ted Hake collection. (T.H.)

Red Ryder and the Western Border Guns
Red Ryder in War on the Range
Red Ryder, the Fighting Westerner
Red Ryder and the Highway Robbers
Red Ryder Brings Law to Devil's Hole

Bobby Benson

The popular Western adventure radio show *Bobby Benson's Adventures* was first heard over CBS in 1932. The program was set on a ranch called the H-Bar-O (after the show's first sponsor, H-O Oats), later renamed the B-Bar-B after Bobby Benson, in the Big Bend country of Texas. The program followed the adventures of Bobby and his pal, Polly, as they fought off the villain Little Snake, the head of a group of Mexican banditos. The show ran from 1932 to 1936; it was revived on Mutual in 1949 as the nation once again became obsessed with cowboy heroes, and ran through 1955. Radio premiums offered include the H-

Bobby Benson's B-Bar-B Riders, *authorized edition coloring book, Whitman, 1950.*

H BAR O RANCH

Autographed 8″ x 10″ photo of Bobby Benson, radio premium sendaway, 1933. Ted Hake collection. (T.H.)

Bar-O Ranger Club button, a code book, a cereal bowl in three different colors, a set of six photographs of Bobby, Polly, and the gang, and a card game. Bobby Benson also appeared in comic-style storybooks such as *Tunnel of Gold* and *The Lost Herd* (both 1936). Actors who played Bobby on the early radio episodes were Richard Wanamaker, Ivan Curry, and Billy Halop. Others included notables Tex Ritter, Al Hodge, and Don Knotts. The show's action was interspersed with western cowboy songs.

Death Valley Days

Another Western radio adventure show that had some premiums connected with it was *Death Valley Days*. It was first aired over the Blue network in September 1930.

In 1944 the program title was changed to *Death Valley Sheriff* and in 1945 to *The Sheriff.* Cowboy collectibles from this show (which had an Old Ranger telling tales of the western terrain as well as doing the Borax commercials) include *The Story of Death Valley* (issued in 1931 and 1932), *The Old Ranger's Yarns of Death Valley* (1933), a 20 Mule-Team jigsaw puzzle (1933), *Death Valley Tales as Told by the Old Ranger* (1934), *Cowboy Songs in Death Valley* (1934), *High Spots of Death Valley Days* Volume 1, #1 (1939), and in the 1950s a model, the 20 Mule-Team and Wagons.

The Cisco Kid

The opening sequence was first heard on the radio in 1943:

PANCHO: Cisco, the sheriff and hees pos-see . . . they are comeeeng closer!

CISCO: This way, Pancho! Vamonos!
(Music up.)
Later it went like this:
CISCO: Of all the señoritas I have known . . . you are the most beautiful.
SEÑORITA: Oh Cisco!
(Music up.)

The Cisco Kid and his sidekick, Pancho, galloped into television in the 1950s. The show would always end with a bad joke followed by:
CISCO: Oh Pancho!
PANCHO: O-o-o-oh Seeeessko!

The Cisco Kid was sponsored by a variety of breads, including Tip-Top, which offered a paper gun called "The Cisco Kid on Television." Comic books were issued by Dell throughout the 1950s, and Saalfield Publishing Co. offered a *Cisco Kid Coloring Book* in 1953.

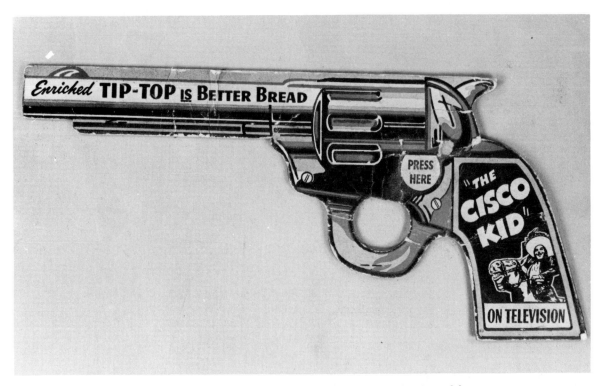

The Cisco Kid on Television, paper gun distributed by Tip Top Bread, c. 1954. Ted Hake collection. (T.H.)

Studio publicity photo of Gene Autry and Champion, 1938.

BACK IN THE SADDLE

The Country Music Hall of Fame elected Gene Autry to its roster of famous musicians in 1969, and the Country Music Association issued a special bronze plaque that read:

America's great singing cowboy paved the way for others with his Western songs on radio and in the movies, where he set box office records. He was among the first country and western performers to win world-wide acclaim. Born a cowboy, he overcame every adversity to move to the top of his field, always lending dignity to the industry. Best known as an artist and actor, he also was an accomplished writer.

The favorite game of kids in England in the late 1940s and early '50s was Cowboys and Indians, just as it was in the States, and when a young English lad named Richard Starkey (later known as Ringo Starr) first heard Gene Autry crooning "South of the Border, Down Mexico Way" he was awestruck and inspired. The famous member of the Beatles recently revealed to host Tom Snyder on the TV interview show *Tomorrow* that he went to see as many Gene Autry movies as he could and said, "I thought calling myself Ringo Starr would be a tribute to Gene, kind of like I was his sidekick, and 'Ringo' has a real 'South of the Border' sound to it, just like Pancho or Cisco. I think Gene Autry is the greatest singer ever." To Ringo Starr, and to millions of other pop country-and-western music fans, Gene Autry still reigns as King of the Singing Cowboys. His singing style, influenced by the late Jimmie Rodgers, set the tone for all of today's Western music. His theme song, "Back in the Saddle Again," written by Autry and Ray Whitley, and another of his big hits, "Take Me Back to My Boots and Saddle," written by Walter Samuels, Leonard Whitcup, and Teddy

Above: *Gene Autry's deluxe edition of famous original* Cowboy Songs and Mountain Ballads, *published by M. M. Cole, 1936. Below: Sheet music for "South of the Border (Down Mexico Way)," published by Peter Maurice Music Co., 1934. (P.C.)*

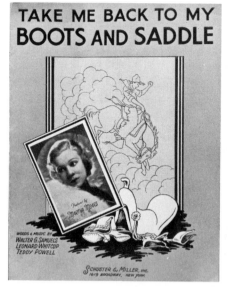 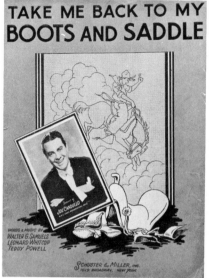 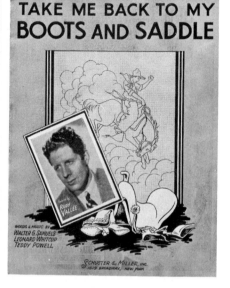

Left to right: *"Take Me Back to My Boots and Saddle," featuring Martha Mears, 1934. (P.C.) "Take Me Back to My Boots and Saddle," featuring Joe Candullo and the NBC Radio Broadcasting Orchestra, 1934. (P.C.) "Take Me Back to My Boots and Saddle," featuring Rudy Vallee, 1934. (P.C.)*

Powell, evoke the nostalgia that is so rampant today for the rustic cowboy life of the Old West. The lyrics sum it all up:

I'm back in the saddle again,
Out where a friend is a friend,
Where the long-horned cattle
feed on the lowly jimson weed.
I'm back in the saddle again.

Ridin' the range once more,
Totin' my old forty-four,
Where you sleep out every night
Where the only law is right
I'm back in the saddle again.

And:

Take me back to my boots and saddle
Ooh-ooh-ooh, ooh-ooh-ooh, ooh-ooh-ooh,
Let me see that gen'ral store,
Let me ride that range once more.
Give me my boots and saddle
Let me ramble along the prairie,
Ooh-ooh-ooh, ooh-ooh-ooh, ooh-ooh-ooh,
Ropin' steers on old "Bar X,"
With my buddies, Slim and Tex,
Give me my boots and saddle.

Other all-time great radio, record, and movie song hits of Gene Autry include:

"Rudolph, the Red-Nosed Reindeer" (at least 10 million copies sold)
"Here Comes Santa Claus"
"You Are My Sunshine"
"Cowboy Blues"
"Goodnight Irene"
"Have I Told You Lately That I Love You?"
"Mexicali Rose"
"South of the Border"
"Sioux City Sue"
"Mule Train"
"Someday You'll Want Me to Want You"
"Buttons and Bows"
"Twilight on the Trail"
"Tumbling Tumbleweeds"
"Tweedle-O-Twill"
"It Happened in Old Monterrey"
"When the Swallows Come Back to Capistrano"
"Maria Elena"
"I Don't Want to Set the World on Fire"

There is a big demand by collectors for song sheets and original recordings of all these hits.

"Back in the Saddle" has become the catch phrase for modern would-be cowboys who wear $300 boots and expensive designer jeans, who lament the passing of the good old cowboy days gone by, and who dance the "Urban Cowboy" shuffle in the countless western-style bars that have popped up from New York to Los Angeles with rough-tough frontier names like Rawhide, Boots, Badlands, the Roundup, Billy the Kid, Boots and Saddles, Cody's, the Lone Star Cafe, and the Old Corral. But most hard-drinking, macho, Johnny Cash urban cowboy types would laugh off Gene Autry's "Ten Cowboy Commandments," which have a ring of rectitude and patriotism that seems too goody-gumdrops for today. This is the "Code of the West" as outlined by Autry for America's movie buckaroos—the kids of the Depression, World War II tots, and 1950s TV kids:

1. He must not take unfair advantage of an enemy.
2. He must never go back on his word.
3. He must always tell the truth.

Gene Autry in Public Cowboy No. 1, *Big Little Book, Whitman, 1938.*

4. He must be gentle with children, elderly people, and animals.
5. He must not possess racially or religiously intolerant ideas.
6. He must help people in distress.
7. He must be a good worker.
8. He must respect women, parents, and his nation's laws.
9. He must neither drink nor smoke.
10. He must be a patriot.

The telegraph office in Chelsea, Oklahoma, was a lonely place; and to pass the hours during the graveyard shift, Orvon Autry strummed and hummed on his guitar. One night, according to legend and Autry himself, Will Rogers sauntered in to send a telegram. After listening to one of his songs, Rogers suggested that Autry go to New York and get himself a job on the radio. Two years later, after achieving wide local popularity as "Oklahoma's Yodeling Cowboy" on Tulsa radio KVOO, Orvon "Gene" Autry signed a contract with the American Record Corporation, which produced records for chain department stores. Autry's first recording session with ARC produced "That Silver-Haired Daddy of Mine," which sold 30,000 copies in the first month of its release in 1930, 300,000 during its initial popularity, and several million copies over the years.

Gene Autry was born in 1907 in Tioga, Texas. His father was a horse trader and cattle dealer who later bought a ranch in Oklahoma, where Gene learned the basic horse- and cattle-handling tricks of the cowboy. It was driving cattle from the

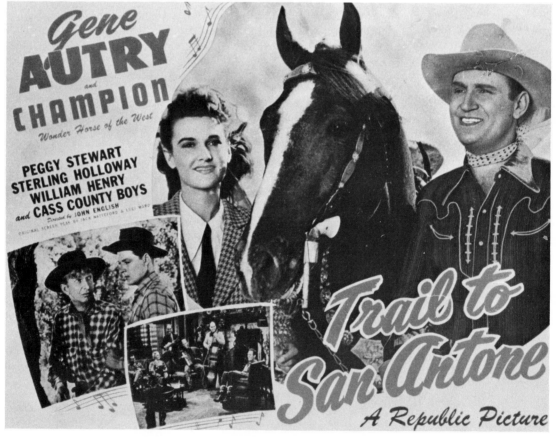

Lobby card for Trail to San Antone, *a Republic picture starring Gene Autry, 1947. (P.C.)*

Melody Ranch Gene Autry lunch box with thermos, both copyright Gene Autry, manufactured by Landers, Frary & Clark of New Britain, Conn., c. 1948.

ranch to the railhead that brought him in contact with the railroads and the telegraph company and to the encouraging words he received from Will Rogers. Sears, Roebuck Company, which provided the major outlet for Gene's Okeh Label recordings through its catalogues and stores, hired him in 1930, and for the next four years, as star of his own *Gene Autry Program* on radio station WLS ("World's Largest Store") in Chicago. He also headlined *The National Barn Dance,* considered to be the first country-and-western radio program, and toured all over a Depression-weary America with the cast of the show. He learned during this time that audiences responded to his shyness and awkwardness and they especially liked that appealing nasal twang in his voice. Will Rogers was beloved for some of these same qualities, and Gene reckoned there would be room for another cowboy from Oklahoma, especially if he could sing.

In 1934 Mascot Pictures had experimented with songs in a couple of Ken Maynard features, and the response had been good. Nat Levine, the producer and head

of Mascot, came up with an offer that led to Gene Autry making his first screen appearance in *In Old Santa Fe,* starring Ken Maynard. Gene, the singing cowboy, was a hit. He was then given his first starring role, in a twelve-chapter serial called *Phantom Empire,* a strange science-fiction Western. He played himself, Gene Autry, a Western radio singer, a good guy who fought against the bad-guy inhabitants of the underground city of Murania. He and his sidekick, Smiley Burnette, always managed to escape from the latest cliff-hanging adventure just in time to meet their broadcast deadline at the "Radio Ranch," where they were at last able to relax and sing their songs, including Gene's hit, "That Silver-Haired Daddy of Mine."

Herbert J. Yates, a former executive of the American Tobacco Company and head of the powerful Consolidated Film Laboratories, cornered the Western film market in 1935 when he established Republic Pictures, a conglomerate of Mascot, Monogram, and Liberty studios. Yates felt he needed something new to bring the Western out of the slump it was in. The success

NEWS WEEKLY • DEC. 5, 1949

Quick

10¢

GENE AUTRY: Richest Cowboy — PAGE 18

Quick *magazine featuring a wealthy cowboy on the cover, December 5, 1949.*

of *Phantom Empire* provided the right formula. Beginning in 1935 with *Tumbling Tumbleweeds* (in which "That Silver-Haired Daddy of Mine" was sung yet again), Gene Autry starred in fifty films over the next ten years, doing for Republic what Tom Mix had done for Fox—becoming a box-office buckaroo bonanza. In 1935 Gene also made *Melody Trail,* singing his own song, "Hold On, Little Doggie, Hold On," *Sagebrush Troubador,* and *The Singing Vagabond.* In 1936 there was *Red River Valley, Comin' Round the Mountain* (featuring "When the Campfire Is Low on the Prairie"), *The Singing Cowboy* ("Rainbow Trail" and "My Old Saddle Pal"), *Guns and Guitars, Oh, Susanna* ("I'll Go Ridin' down That Old Texas Trail"), *Ride, Ranger, Ride, The Big Show* (the backup singing group in this film was the Sons of the Pioneers with Dick Weston, later known as Roy Rogers), and *The Old Corral,* featuring the songs "So Long Old Paint" and "In the Heart of the West."

The formula was always the same: Gene was the singing cowboy, always playing himself, with his "World's Wonder Horse," Champion, and comic sidekick, Smiley "Frog" Burnette, outmanuevering the bad guys (who usually drove old Packards while Gene and the good guys used Hudson Hornets and Studebakers), wooing the pretty leading ladies (who played hard-to-get so that Gene would have to sing more songs), and always heading back to the ranch to sing another song in front of the campfire. Gene's acting ability was limited; he didn't even really look like a cowboy, being overweight and unathletic. Autry said of himself, "I'm not a great actor; I'm not a great rider; I'm not a great singer; but what the hell is my opinion when fifty million people think I do pretty good?" sounding like an echo of his patron saint, Will Rogers.

Acting ability, charm, and popularity aside, by 1937 Gene Autry had made over twenty pictures for Republic and was still averaging a salary of about $150 per week. Republic was riding high with the success of the Gene Autry Westerns, but Herbert J. Yates wasn't interested in negotiating a new contract. He threatened Gene with a new singing cowboy, Roy Rogers. Gene finally just walked out on Republic. Yates soon found that he couldn't sell any Republic movies at all to distributors without throwing in at least one or two of the Autry pictures to round out the deal, so he finally capitulated and raised Autry's salary to $12,500 for each film, with six to eight films to be made per year.

Gene Autry's feature films in 1937 included *Roundup Time in Texas, Git Along, Little Doggies, Yodelin' Kid from Pine Ridge* ("Sing Me a Song of the Saddle"), *Public Cowboy No. 1* ("The West Ain't What It Used to Be"), *Boots and Saddles,* and *Springtime in the Rockies.* By 1939 the Autry formula was set; *Mexicali Rose,* which included the title song and

"You're the Only Star in My Blue Heaven," blended action, music, comedy, and sentimentality. *South of the Border,* Ringo Starr's favorite, had a title song that became a standard on two continents. *Melody Ranch,* made in 1940, was named after Gene's popular radio show and featured Ann Miller, Jimmy Durante, and George "Gabby" Hayes. In 1940 Gene Autry was the fourth-ranking of the top ten moneymaking stars in Hollywood, following Mickey Rooney, Spencer Tracy, and Clark Gable. From 1937 to 1942 he placed first in the Motion Picture Herald Poll of Top Moneymaking Western Stars. One of the last pictures Autry made before going off to World War II was *Stardust on the Trail,* which had so many songs there was no time for story line, romance, or action. The songs included "When Roses Bloom Again," "Wouldn't You Like to Know,"

"Home on the Range," "Deep in the Heart of Texas," "Roll on Little Doggies," and "You Are My Sunshine."

After the war Gene formed his own company to produce films for Columbia (thirty films from 1947 to 1953, the last one being *Last of the Pony Riders*), upped his personal appearance schedule (once grossing $800,000 in two months), and started paying more attention to linking his name with more than forty products, which by the late 1940s were paying him $100,000 per year in royalties. At that time he was making $5,000 a week on the radio alone. The half-hour *Melody Ranch* radio show was first heard in January 1940 on CBS on Sunday afternoons, and later on Saturday evenings. The program was a Western adventure, interspersed with interludes of music, and featured Pat Buttram (Gene's radio and postwar film sidekick), Jim

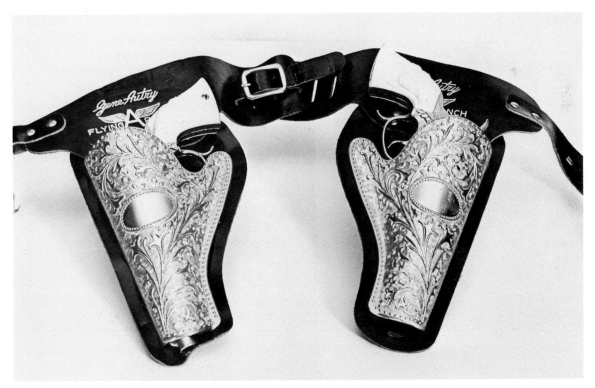

Gene Autry Flying "A" two-gun holster set,
c. 1950. Ted Hake collection.

Boles, and Tyler McVey. The Cass County Boys (a trio led by Carl Cotner), the King Sisters, and Mary Ford (later of Les Paul and Mary Ford) provided the backup music. The announcer was Lou Crosby, who intoned, "Where the pavement ends the West begins." Wrigley Chewing Gum was the sponsor of the highly regarded *Melody Ranch* show until it left the air in 1956. "Its easy chewing makes those little jobs go a little easier. I like it," Crosby would proclaim.

The richest cowboy in the world had a number of business ventures—radio stations, newspapers, oil wells, cattle ranches,

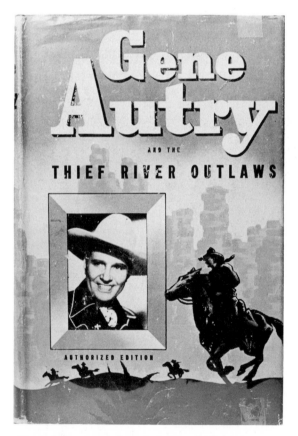

Gene Autry and the Thief River Outlaws, *by Bob Hamilton, with illustrations by Dan Muller, authorized edition published by Whitman, 1944.*

a flying school, a traveling rodeo, two song-publishing companies, a publishing company putting out 100,000 Gene Autry comic books a month, a baseball team, and a chain of movie theaters. In the early 1950s he was the first movie cowboy star to make half-hour Western films especially for television. His company, Flying "A" Productions, ground out eighty-five *Gene Autry* shows, seventy-six episodes of *The Range Rider,* with Jock Mahoney, the first thirty-nine episodes of *Death Valley Days,* with Stanley Andrews as the Old Ranger, eighty sequences of *Annie Oakley,* starring Gail Davis, forty *Buffalo Bill Jr.* shows, and *Champion—The Story of a Wild Stallion, a 12-Year-Old Boy and His Dog Rebel.* These series started going into reruns after 1954.

Gene Autry did not make any films, do any television acting, or make any recordings after the early 1950s. He concentrated on his business ventures and quietly settled down into a comfortable semiretirement after all the excitement and hoopla of his movie-star cowboy years. The people of Tioga, Texas, renamed it Autry Springs to show their love for the enormously successful and world-renowned singing cowboy who lived there and who had one of the most important ingredients it takes to become an American hero—the common touch.

GENE AUTRY COLLECTIBLES

Gene Autry comics were originally published by Fawcett in 1941 and continued through 1946. Issue #1 (extremely rare) through issue #10 are the best of the Autry comic collectibles. In 1946 Dell took over publication, started a new numbering system, and continued up to 1959 with #121 the final issue. March of Comics, published by K. K. Publications/Western Publishing Company, issued a number of Gene Autry

Quaker Puffed Sparkies magazine advertisement, late 1940s.

Above: *Official Gene Autry Ranch Outfit, including chaps, vest, shirt, neckerchief, lariat, and hat, manufactured by M. A. Henry Co., 1941. Below: Gene Autry Official Ranch Outfit box, 1941.*

titles, including issues #25, 28, 39, 54, 78, 90, 104, 120, 135, and 150. These were giveaways with glossy back covers for advertisers. In 1947 Pillsbury issued a 32-page premium comic book titled *Gene Autry Adventure Comics and Play-Fun Book*, which included games, comics, and puzzles. In 1950 five different 2½″ x 6¾″ giveaways were issued under the title *Phantom of the Cave*. In 1953 a 3-D giveaway pocket-size comic book was issued. Gene Autry's *Champion* was published from 1950 to 1955.

Throughout the late 1930s and into the 1950s, Whitman Publishing Company issued the following Big Little Books and Better Little Books:

Gene Autry and the Land Grab Mystery
Gene Autry and the Mystery of Paint Rock Canyon
Gene Autry and the Range War
Gene Autry and the Red Bandit's Ghost
Gene Autry, Cowboy Detective
Gene Autry in Law of the Range
Gene Autry in Public Cowboy No. 1
Gene Autry in Special Range Rule
Gene Autry in Gunsmoke
Gene Autry and the Bandits at Silver Tip
Gene Autry in Hawk of the Hills
Gene Autry in Raiders of the Range
Gene Autry, Special Ranger

During the 1940s and '50s Whitman also published hardcover adventure books for young adults, which included the following titles:

Thief River Outlaws
Big Valley Grab
The Redwood Pirates
Golden Stallion
Arapaho War Drums

In 1941 Merrill Publishing Company produced the first Gene Autry *Cowboy Adventures to Color* in a 10″ x 15″ format. This was followed in 1950 and 1951 with

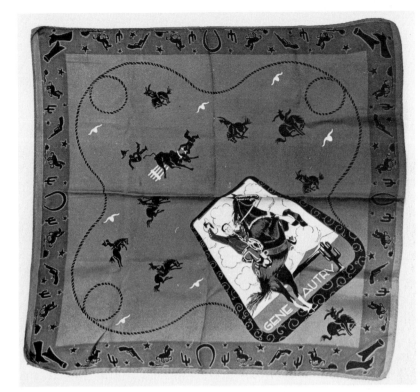

*Gene Autry satin-rayon neckerchief.
Ted Hake collection.*

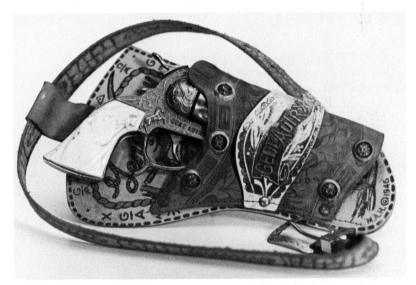

*Leather holster dated 1946.
Metal Gene Autry cap gun
with pearled handle. Ted Hake
collection.*

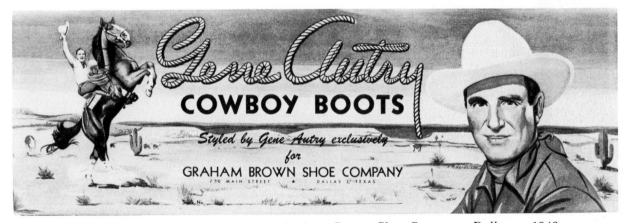

Label for Gene Autry Cowboy Boots, Graham Brown Shoe Company, Dallas, c. 1946.

Red and white Gene Autry rubber children's galoshes, c. 1950. Ted Hake collection.

Whitman's *Gene Autry Coloring Book* in an 11" x 15" format. In 1950 Whitman published the *Melody Ranch Cut-Out Dolls* and in 1953 the *Chuck Wagon Chatter Coloring Book.* Gene Autry song sheets are excellent collectibles with handsome graphics quite suitable for framing. Song books include the 1934 *Oklahoma Yodeling Cowboy—Gene Autry's Famous Cowboy Songs and Mountain Ballads,* with 64 pages, published by M. M. Cole Publishing Company of Chicago, and *Songs Gene Autry Sings,* published in 1942 by the Western Music Publishing Company. During the war Sergeant Gene Autry presented his favorite patriotic and hillbilly songs in a songbook with a picture of himself on the cover. Columbia issued several 78-rpm record albums; the *Picture Story* albums included illustrations and words to sing along with.

Gene Autry wristwatch, Wilane Watch Co., dated 1948. This watch originally sold for $6.95. Robert Lesser collection.

There was plenty of other merchandise: a colorful Gene Autry scarf, elastic western braces, a Melody Ranch thermos bottle and lunch box, six-shooter sets, cap pistols, pencil tablets, and stencil books. Numerous "autographed" photos of Gene and Champion could be had by sending away to Quaker Puffed Wheat and Rice, who offered comic premiums, or Sunbeam Bread, who offered a blue pinback button claiming it was "Gene Autry's Brand." Ralston had a portrait ring, one in a series that included Orphan Annie, Dick Tracy, and Frank Buck. There were holster sets, sweatshirts, games, hair oils, spurs, chaps, and the Autry Stampede Suit, promoted as "Western Made for Western Man."

The Wilane Watch Company produced the first Gene Autry and Champion wristwatch in 1935, with bright colors and "radium" hands to tell time in the dark. In 1948 Wilane redesigned the watch and included a cowboy wristband and an inscription embossed on the back: "Always your pal, Gene Autry." This watch was quite successful and was redesigned once again in 1951, this time with animation. It was called the Six-Shooter, and the second hand became a six-gun that rocked back and forth and fired "120 shots a minute." This watch was manufactured by the New Haven Watch and Clock Company.

In 1949 Monarch manufactured the Gene Autry Bicycle. It had balloon tires, a horse's head between the handles, a holster and gun set, and a pseudo-saddle, and was encrusted all over with glass jewels. Because Gene would not go onto television to publicize the bike, it did not sell and was completely overshadowed by the enormously successful Hopalong Cassidy Bicycle. Only approximately 2,500 of the Gene Autry bikes were made, making them quite rare indeed. This would be considered the ultimate Autry cowboy dream collectible.

Gene Autry and Champion wristwatch, manufactured by the Wilane Watch Company, c. 1935. Robert Lesser collection.

Movie Life magazine featuring Roy Rogers, Dale Evans, and their children on the cover, November 1948.

HAPPY TRAILS TO YOU

I am writing this in my portable dressing room at Republic Studios, where we are shooting *Susanna Pass*. Right next door is the dressing room of the girl who is playing opposite me in the picture and—what do you know?—once more she's Dale Evans. It's just like old times.

Roy Rogers made this comment in *Modern Screen* magazine in 1949, after Republic Studios had relented on its decision to separate Roy and Dale as a romantic team in the *King of the Cowboys* Western series. He continued:

It fits right into the plan of life we'd talked about when we were married—the plan the studio busted all to bits when it decided that a married couple made a poor romantic team on the screen. And, in addition to Dale and myself, there are three other members of our family who are plumb delighted: Cheryl, our oldest, who's eight, Linda Lou, who's five; and Roy Jr., who's 27 months old and whom we call "Dusty" on account of he generally is. All five of us are deeply grateful to the thousands of fans who wrote us at Republic and convinced the studio that it was wrong about separating us. That plan Dale and I made when we married a year ago was centered around our home. We decided we'd guide our careers so we could spend as much time as possible together—as a family.

Yes sir, it's just like old times—and I'm sure thankful to the fans, to *Modern Screen,* and to everyone who brought my Dale back to me. Just think—three and a half years, up to the time of our marriage, we made 24 pictures together! I don't have to tell you that we got so we could sail through a scene, no matter how tough it was, because we were comfortable with each other, knew just how the other worked. And then, just because we moved even closer together in our personal lives, we had to split up professionally! But that's all over now. I'm a happy man again. Dale is right next to me—and all I have to do is look through the window to see Old Trigger tied to a post.

There was a postscript from Dale:

I knew it! I knew he'd have to get his Old Trigger into this somewhere.

So the movie fans of the 1940s were brought into some of the personal and professional ups and downs of America's ideal cowboy-cowgirl couple. Whenever Roy and Dale are mentioned, wherever they go together or individually, they have become synonymous with all the good virtues of the American family, possessing high moral standards, a specific relationship with God and with country, and above and beyond all of this, fame and financial success.

Roy Rogers had a rustic upbringing. Born in 1911 in Duck Run, Ohio, he worked a small farm with his mother and sisters while his father labored at the U.S. Shoe Company in Cincinnati. He was a member of the 4-H Club and raised a fancy blue-ribbon pig named Martha Washington. He also learned to play the guitar and became the best square-dance caller in Duck Run. Hard times forced the Slye family (Roy's pre-Hollywood name was Leonard Slye) to give up the farm, so then Roy went to work at the shoe factory also. He and his father slaved away at this monotony, despising every minute of it, until one day in the summer of 1929 Roy's father said, "Leonard, let's go out and see Mary tomorrow." Mary was Roy's sister, who had married and moved to Lawndale, California. They jumped into the old family Dodge and drove to California, where Roy managed to find a job driving dump trucks and picking peaches with the Okies. It was heavy work, but Roy loved the sunny openness of California and became determined to make a new life for himself.

He spent a great deal of his extra time strumming on his guitar, eventually getting up enough nerve to perform on a radio amateur show called *Midnight Frolic*. Shortly after that stint he was asked to join up with a group of country musicians called the Rocky Mountaineers as lead vocalist on weekly radio programs. There was little money to be made, but this marked the beginnings of a show-business career for Roy Rogers. Like a lot of other cowboy types in Southern California during the early years of the Depression, Roy yearned to break into the big time of movies and entertainment. The group disbanded, and Roy formed another, called the International Cowboys. These boys initially performed on the radio for no pay, but eventually they were hired for a barnstorming tour throughout the Southwest. Changing the group's name to the O-Bar-O Cowboys, they hit the trail on a musical tour which took them to Yuma, Arizona; Miami, Arizona; Lubbock, Texas; and Roswell, New Mexico. The tour did not bring the boys success, and by the time they reached Roswell they were flat broke. However, they managed to land a spot on a local radio station, which paid them enough for lodging expenses though they remained good and hungry; according to Roy, between their musical numbers they would talk about what they would like to be eating. Roy liked lemon meringue pies, another musician preferred chicken, and another biscuits; and they talked about this over the airwaves. Arlene Wilkins, a pretty girl who lived with her family in Roswell, listened to the cowboy singing group on the radio each day because she loved to hear them yodel. One evening her brother called up the radio station and said that if the boys would dedicate a yodeling number to his sister Arlene and say her name "right out plain" on the air, she would make them a lemon meringue pie. Roy practiced his high-yell yodeling that night, and the next day, after performing on the radio, he was visited by Arlene and her mother, carrying two large lemon pies topped with billowing meringue. Arlene apparently batted her eyelashes at Roy, and he was elected by the boys in the band to return her pie plates. Three years later, though a shy and blushing cowboy, Roy proposed to the fair Ar-

lene, marrying her after a performance at the Texas Centennial in Dallas in 1936. By this time he was almost big-time by Depression standards, making $35 a week singing with a group called the Sons of the Pioneers. As far as Roy was concerned this was enough money, and he felt it was time he and Arlene started a family.

The Sons of the Pioneers was considered a hot group by 1936, having made film appearances in 1935 in *The Old Homestead* and in *Tumbling Tumbleweeds,* in which Gene Autry had his first starring role. In 1936 they signed a record contract with Decca and appeared in two more tuneful Gene Autry Westerns, *The Big Show* and *The Old Corral.* The same year they were seen in a Columbia film, *The Mysterious Avenger* starring Charles Starrett, and they did a bit in a "prestige" Western, *Rhythm on the Range,* starring crooner Bing Crosby and beautiful, blond, sultry Frances Farmer.

One day in 1937 Roy was in a hat shop having his big white Stetson cleaned and blocked. An actor bolted in, saying he needed a rush cleanup job on his cowboy hat because they were having auditions for singing cowboys over at Republic Studios the next day. Having overheard this, Roy went sneaking in through the studio gates and bumped into the man doing the auditioning. "Can you sing?" demanded Sol Siegel, a Republic executive. Roy gulped out a "yes," made an audition date for later that morning, and ran home full speed to fetch his guitar. Siegel had heard seventeen other prospective cowboys that morning, but somehow Roy's authentic western range songs, which included a lot of yip and yodeling, impressed him. Roy got not only a movie contract and a preliminary screen test but also a new Hollywood name—Dick Weston.

Roy Rogers has often been asked how he first got into the picture business; and he

Roy Rogers and Trigger decal appliqué by Meyercord, c. 1950.

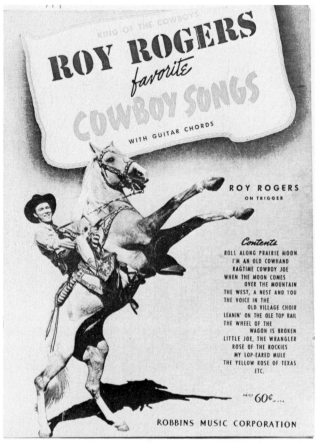

Above: Roy Rogers Favorite Cowboy Songs, *song folio, Robbins Music Corp., 1943. Be-low: RCA Victor 2-record set, "Lore of the West," starring Roy Rogers with sidekick Gabby Hayes and Trigger, and containing a 12-page illustrated storybook of cowboy defi-nitions, words and music by Country Wash-burne and Foster Carling, 1949.*

always answers that God must have wanted him to, otherwise He wouldn't have set up all the details that dovetailed into the au-dition for Republic. This may be true, but if so it was also the president of Republic Studios, Herbert J. Yates, a feisty, very mortal mogul, who tipped the scales. Gene Autry, by 1938 the top box-office cowboy in the country, was demanding more mon-ey and deliberately took off from Holly-wood on an "extended leave" just before work on a new picture was to begin. Yates stubbornly refused to raise his salary; in-stead he sent out a call for a new singing cowboy. Dick Weston was ready, willing, and able when he was called in to star in the new Republic feature, *Under Western Stars.* The producers had a conference and decided on a big budget; they hired Smiley Burnette as Roy's sidekick, and someone in the publicity department came up with an-other new name for the new star—Roy Rogers. Roy took on the task of auditioning his own horse. When he rode a particularly beautiful palomino named Golden Cloud, whose sire was a racehorse at Caliente, he knew he had found just the right one for his taste and new image. He bought the horse for $2,500. This one was a fast horse, Roy thought, quick as a . . . Trigger! And that was the name Roy gave him. Trigger was the "smartest horse in the movies." He could count up to 25 by stamping his hoof, and he also did simple subtraction and multiplication. He drank milk out of a bot-tle by himself, signed his own "X" on hotel registers, and walked 150 feet on his hind legs. Trigger's best trick though, it was said, was practicing self-restraint indoors.

Roy Rogers's first film went over well with critics and public alike, and between 1938 and 1942 he made thirty-six features for Republic. They were different from Gene Autry's modern Westerns in that they were historical, set in the period of the real cowboy of the 1870s. They also in-

Lobby card from Roy Rogers film
Song of Arizona, *1946. (P.C.)*

Roy Rogers "King of the Cowboys" silk scarf,
featuring Roy, Trigger, and Bullet, c. 1945.

cluded only two or three songs per film, compared with the five to eight Gene always sang in his features. Unlike Gene, Roy never played himself, always choosing instead to portray characters like Billy the Kid, Buffalo Bill, Wild Bill Hickok, or sometimes just plain cowpokes. Roy Rogers films became very popular in small-town and rural America, which was the economic backbone for Western movie producers like Republic. It has been noted that the 410 black movie houses existing in America during the late 1930s and early '40s were also big customers of the Western film. But Roy's popularity lagged behind Gene's until Gene went off to war.

It seemed that whenever Gene Autry left town, Roy Rogers started stalking and taking over his movie cowboy territory. When Gene "defected" to the Army Air Corps, as Herbert Yates expressed it, the Republic Pictures publicity department proclaimed Roy Rogers "King of the Cowboys" on orders from the boss. Republic launched a massive promotional campaign and increased the budgets on Roy's Westerns to $350,000 per picture, with big advertising campaigns. Yates invested more money in promoting Roy Rogers than he did even for his own special favorite protégé star, Vera Hruba Ralston, who, when she was not on ice skates, was sometimes obliged to ride a horse.

In 1944 Roy made *The Cowboy and the*

Lobby card from 1945 film Utah, *featuring Roy and his pretty co-star Dale Evans. (P.C.)*

Señorita, which co-starred Dale Evans. Dale, who hailed out of Texas and whose real name was Frances Smith, had performed as a radio singer, notably on Edgar Bergen and Charlie McCarthy's *Chase and Sanborn Hour.* She had appeared in *Swing Your Partner* in 1943 and was doing bit parts and recording popular hits. Yates chose her for the Señorita role and signed her for the next twenty consecutive Roy Rogers Westerns. In 1946 Roy's wife, Arlene, died shortly after giving birth to their second child; and a year later a lonely cowboy star married his leading lady, the lovely Dale Evans. The series always co-starred George "Gabby" Hayes or Andy Devine or Pat Brady as the constant sidekicks, Dale Evans as "The Queen of the West," and Trigger, who appeared in all ninety of Roy's films. Roy's old musical group, the Sons of the Pioneers, was also featured. Some of the films, which reflect Herbert Yates's penchant for using the names of states in titles, were *Idaho, Song of Texas, Song of Nevada, Rainbow over Texas, Song of Arizona, Utah, The Man from Oklahoma, Colorado, Under California Skies,* and *Down Dakota Way.* Other Roy Rogers films were *Billy the Kid Returns, Wall Street Cowboy, Days of Jesse James, Young Buffalo Bill, The Dark Command* (with Claire Trevor and John Wayne), *Young Bill Hickok, In Old Cheyenne, Sheriff of Tombstone, Red River Valley, Romance on the Range, Sons of the Pioneers, The Yellow Rose of Texas, Hollywood Canteen* (a guest appearance with Trigger, where he sang Cole Porter's "Don't Fence Me In"), *My Pal Trigger, The Gay Ranchero,* and his last film for Republic in 1951, *Pals of the Golden West.* In 1952 he appeared with Bob Hope and Jane Russell in Paramount's *Son of Paleface.* This was Roy's last movie, except for a brief guest appearance in Bob Hope's 1959 comedy, *Alias Jesse James.*

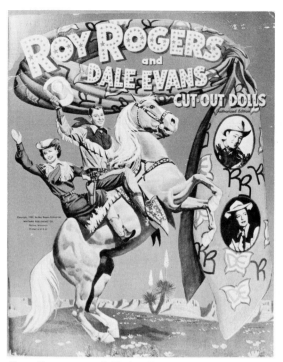

Roy Rogers and Dale Evans cut-out dolls, Whitman, 1952. Below: *Western clothes from a cut-out doll book, featuring Dale Evans, who was often referred to as "Queen of the West." Whitman, 1952. (P.C.)*

"Flash Cowboy" Roy Rogers featured in The Raiders of Sawtooth Ridge, *by Snowden Miller, hardcover with dust jacket, illustrations by Henry Vallely, authorized edition published by Whitman, 1946. (P.C.)*

Roy Rogers is a true cowboy hero in every sense. He doesn't drink much, smoke, or shoot pool, he never spits and never can be heard using "cuss" words other than an occasional "shucks." He likes to be clean-shaven, and he is a real "flash cowboy" clothes horse, wearing whipcord jackets and pants, suede-fringe shirts, and hand-tooled boots and belt and sporting multi-colored kerchiefs, some with his name emblazoned on them. (Roy Rogers lent his name to clothing manufacturers long before Gloria Vanderbilt ever thought of it.)

In 1944 Goodyear Tire and Rubber sponsored the *Roy Rogers* radio show, featuring music and Western adventure. In 1948 the program starred Roy and Dale and Foy Willing and the Riders of the Purple Sage, sponsored by Quaker Oats and Mother's Oats. The theme was "Smiles Are Made out of Sunshine," and the show's commercial jingle had such American cowboy breakfast cereal lines as "Delicious, nutritious, makes you ambitious." The theme song became "It's Roundup Time on the Double-R-Bar" when Post Sugar Crisps became the sponsor, and Pat Brady replaced Gabby Hayes. Dodge Automobile was the sponsor from 1953 to 1955, and the show's theme song became "Happy Trails." This is the song most closely associated with Roy and Dale. "Happy Trails" opens with Trigger-like hoofbeats and Roy's whistling, and is a likable Western song sung in a sunny-prairie style by the happy Mr. and Mrs. duo.

At the height of his popularity in 1943, Roy Rogers began receiving requests for commercial tie-ups for cap guns, T-shirts, and other merchandise. He was fortunate that his boss, Herbert J. Yates, was a penny-pincher who always held people to their contract unto the letter of the finest print. Yates consistently refused to give Rogers the raise in salary he so justly deserved, just as he had done with Gene Autry. Both men had made a fortune for Yates. Roy had his lawyer draw up a contract giving him the commercial rights to his own name, voice, and likeness. Yates signed the contract tongue-in-cheek, relieved at not having to fork over money. For Roy it became a windfall. At one point in the early 1940s he was second only to Walt Disney with the number of products bearing his endorsement. By the mid-1950s, after his television program had gone on the air and attracted a whole new generation of fans, Roy Rogers merchandise earned over $33 million.

When Roy decided that the time had come to go into television, just as his competitor pals Gene Autry and Hopalong Cassidy had, he got socked by the iron hand of Herbert Yates again. Yates intended to sell Roy's movies to television; Roy felt that they would compete with a TV series. Roy's lawyer took Republic to court, trying to bar Republic's sales, claiming Roy owned 100 percent of his name, voice, and likeness and that this also should apply to his films. The movie-mogul vs. star-in-the-saddle battle raged for three years; a lower

court at one point disallowed Republic's right to sell Roy Rogers films to television; finally a higher court reversed the decision. Yates and Republic made millions through the little box that entered the living rooms of America, but so did Roy Rogers. General Foods, his television sponsor, went ahead with the filming of 107 episodes in the *Roy Rogers* series; and this series became enormously popular, adding more and more money to Roy and Dale's Hollywood ranch

Roy Rogers and Dale Evans "Double R Bar Ranch" lunch box and thermos bottle, manufactured by the American Thermos Bottle Co., Norwich, Conn., c. 1948.

Roy Rogers Hauler and Van Trailer with Nellybelle Jeep and plastic toy figures, Marx, c. 1955. Fred Orlansky collection.

lifestyle than they—or God—had ever imagined. The TV show's format had Roy playing the role of the owner of the Double-R-Bar Ranch, located in Paradise Valley. Dale rode a new filly called Buttermilk (who replaced Pal, her movie horse, whom producers felt looked too much like Trigger on the small TV screen), and Pat Brady was the slapstick sidekick who drove a jeep called Nellybelle. And there was a new wonder animal: Bullet, "The Wonder Dog," was added to the Double-R-Bar Ranch stable, replacing Roy's movie dog, Spur. The series ran on NBC throughout the 1950s and into reruns in the 1960s.

Somewhere in the mid-1950s "deep religious feelings" began to emerge in Roy and Dale. Having lost three of their children to sickness or accident, they both turned to God for relief and renewed faith in a life

that so often dealt tragedy in the face of all that was good. Both became apostles of the faith; at rodeos and circuses, during personal appearances on TV and radio, and at church conferences, they would relate some kind of message or testimonial to a captive audience. Under a shaft of golden light that appeared to be one of the sunbeams from "Happy Trails," Roy Rogers would preach to young aspiring cowboys and cowgirls on the importance of the Bible's teachings, Sunday school, and their bedtime prayers. With Trigger himself kneeling in prayer alongside his earthly master, Roy would sing "Peace in the Valley." Dale has written several faith-awakening religious books and has spoken at religious retreats to primarily white middle- or lower-class Protestant audiences. Most of the couple's TV appearances have been on crusades or religious revivals led by evange-

Roy Rogers and Trigger Signal Siren flashlight with secret code and original box, Usalite, c. 1948. Ted Hake collection.

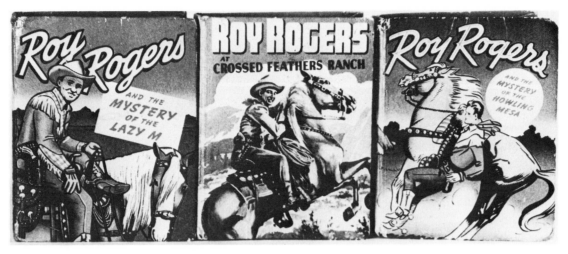

Three Better Little Books by Whitman: Roy Rogers and the Mystery of the Lazy M, *1949;* Roy Rogers at Crossed Feathers Ranch, *1945; and* Roy Rogers and the Mystery of the Howling Mesa, *1948. (P.C.)*

lists Billy Graham or Oral Roberts. The Roy Rogers–Dale Evans union has inspired other western-style couples, such as Nancy and Ronald Reagan, to pronounce to Americans their responsibility to search for a higher morality set by their own example.

After moving to Apple Valley, California, Roy, Dale, and the family proudly opened the Roy Rogers Museum, which features a gigantic statue of Trigger rearing up over the entrance. Roy also had Trigger immortalized by a taxidermist. In 1976 a new museum site was opened in Victorville, a short distance away, featuring Trigger, Buttermilk, Bullet, and Trigger Jr., all stuffed, posed in one of their famous dance routines. Other memorabilia, including photos and collectibles abound, all saved for posterity by Roy and Dale.

ROY ROGERS COLLECTIBLES

Roy Rogers's radio show was quite popular in the late 1940s, and when Quaker Oats became the sponsor in 1948, they issued a large variety of premiums to send away for, including a branding iron ring, a sterling silver hat ring that was signed across the brim, a microscope ring, a deputy star

badge with a secret compartment and a whistle on the back, and a plastic toby mug of Roy. In the early 1950s, Quaker Oats offered a week with Roy Rogers as first prize (with 22,501 other "exciting Western prizes" as consolation) to the boy or girl who came up with a name for Trigger's son (he was eventually called Trigger, Jr.). Another contest had Roy saying, "Win this big chance to be in my next movie." It is not recorded whether any young hopeful won this contest, although a boy named Dusty appeared in the Roy Rogers TV series.

In 1952 Post Cereals became the sponsor, and they issued a number of "in-pack" items that you could get simply by buying the cereal. A Riders Club was established, for which a number of items were needed to qualify you as a bona fide member in good standing, including the Club card, the Club tab (for your collar button), the membership lucky coin, which you attached to your key chain, the official Riders Club comics, and various color photos of Roy and Trigger. There were thirty-six Post "pop-out" cards, and twenty-seven Post Raisin Bran Western medals. The cereal company also issued a thin tin ring of Roy

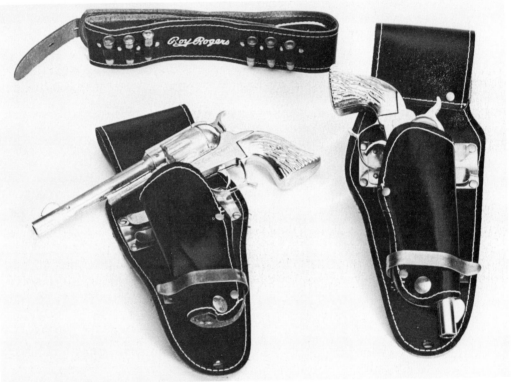

Top left: *Genuine Cowhide Roy Rogers Official Flash-Draw Holster Outfit features swivel holsters and two guns, c. 1948. Ted Hake collection. Above: Roy Rogers gun and holster set with cartridge belt and bullets. Ted Hake collection. Left: Roy Rogers and Trigger official Holster Outfit box, Classy Products, N.Y., c. 1948.*

and one of Trigger, which you had to wrap around your finger.

The March of Comics issued twenty-five special Roy Rogers titles from 1948 through the 1960s. Dell published *Roy Rogers* comics from 1944 into the late 1950s, including a special Dodge giveaway comic called *Roy Rogers and the Man from Dodge City*. In 1955 the comic series title was changed to *Roy Rogers and Trigger*, and Trigger had his own comic from 1951 to 1955. Dale Evans had two publishers: *Dale Evans* comics were published from 1948 to 1952 by National Periodical Publications, and *Queen of the West, Dale Evans*, was published from 1953 to 1959 by Dell.

Whitman issued its first Roy Rogers Bet-

ter Little Book, *Roy Rogers, King of the Cowboys*, in 1943 in conjunction with the release of *King of the Cowboys*, Roy's first "bigger" budget Western. Other Better Little Books were:

Roy Rogers at Crossed Feathers Ranch
Roy Rogers and the Deadly Treasure
Roy Rogers and the Dwarf-Cattle Ranch
Roy Rogers and the Mystery of the Howling Mesa
Roy Rogers and the Mystery of the Lazy M
Roy Rogers in Robbers Roost
Roy Rogers, Robin Hood of the Range

There were two Tall Better Little Books, *Roy Rogers, Range Detective* and *Roy Rogers and the Snowbound Outlaws*. Hardcover Whitman illustrated novels were *Roy*

"The smallest cap firing pistol in the world!"—2" Roy Rogers Tuck-A-Way Gun, on original card, c. 1950. (P.C.)

Rogers and the Gopher Creek Gunman (1945) and *Roy Rogers and the Raiders of Sawtooth Ridge* (1946). The books issued without dust jackets were *The Enchanted Canyon* (1954) and *The Brasada Bandits* (1955). In 1952 Whitman issued *Sure 'Nough Cowpoke,* a "Tell-a-Tale" hardcover book with 28 pages. Whitman published a *Roy Rogers Paint Book* in 1944; Roy Rogers and Dale Evans cut-out doll books in 1952, 1953, 1954, and 1956; "punch-out" books in 1952 and 1954; and jigsaw puzzles in 1952, 1953, and 1957. Also in 1957 Whitman issued a Roy and Dale *and* Dusty cut-out doll. Simon and Schuster published a Big Golden Book hardcover called *King of the Cowboys* in 1953.

Roy Rogers' Own Songs, Folio #1 was published by American Music, and Robbins Music came out with *Roy Rogers' Favorite Cowboy Songs,* a 72-page book, both 1943. In the 1950s, as part of the *Little Nipper Story Book Album* series, RCA Victor issued two 2-record albums with stories and pictures, *Lore of the West* and *Roy Rogers Tells and Sings About Pecos Bill,* the mythological cowboy hero who "dug rivers with a stick, shot down stars with his six-shooter and was the toughest critter West of the Alamo." This album was made in conjunction with Walt Disney's film *Melody Time,* in which Pecos Bill was a leading character.

Usable Roy Rogers collectibles include a 12″-high Many Happy Trails plaster lamp, Roy Rogers and Trigger bandannas, hand-shape washcloths, white ceramic mugs with color pictures, and a Double-R-Bar Ranch lunch box with a Roy Rogers and Dale Evans thermos bottle. There was also a Chow Wagon lunch box. Yankiboy Play Clothes offered the first Official Cowboy Outfit in the mid-1940s; it had a pair of chaps, a vest, a cowboy shirt, a scarf, and a pair of spurs with bells. There were Trigger and

Roy slip-on boots available; and Plus Brand offered a "genuine leather" holster set, which included Roy Rogers's Pledge to Parents: "Dale and I are very proud of every product that bears our name, and we use these items for our own children. You pay no premium for our name. Rather, it is your assurance of authenticity and quality."

The Roy Rogers Official Flash-Draw Holster Outfit had a swivel holster so you could shoot without unholstering your gun. Marx Toy Company issued a Cap Shooting Carbine Rifle; George Schmidt offered a boxed set of spurs. Other collectibles include:

Roy Rogers and Trigger toy guitar
Signal Siren flashlight by Usalite
camera by Herbert George Company
modeling clay set with Roy Rogers molds and sculpture pictures
Ranch lantern by the Ohio Art Company
painted white metal boot-shaped bank
Western Communicating Telephone set run by batteries
cowboy band set of plastic musical instruments
pencil box
pocket knives
pin-back multicolor tin buttons
celluloid buttons
white metal badges

Republic issued dozens of color and black-and-white publicity stills of Roy and Trigger and Dale. Ingraham produced an animated Roy Rogers and Trigger alarm clock in 1951 and two wristwatches: the first had a square case with Roy on a rearing Trigger; the second, a round case with Roy holding Trigger's nose. Bradley Time Company produced a Queen of the West Dale Evans wristwatch in a celluloid-enclosed pop-up box. Bradley also produced a Roy Rogers pocket watch in the late 1950s, with a stop-watch feature.

Roy Rogers 40-hour wind-up alarm clock with an animated Roy Rogers "riding" on Trigger, produced by Ingraham Company, Bristol, Conn., 1951. This clock sold for $4.14. Below, left: Roy Rogers and Trigger pocket watch produced by Bradley, 1959. Robert Lesser collection. Right: Dale Evans wristwatch, Ingraham, 1951.

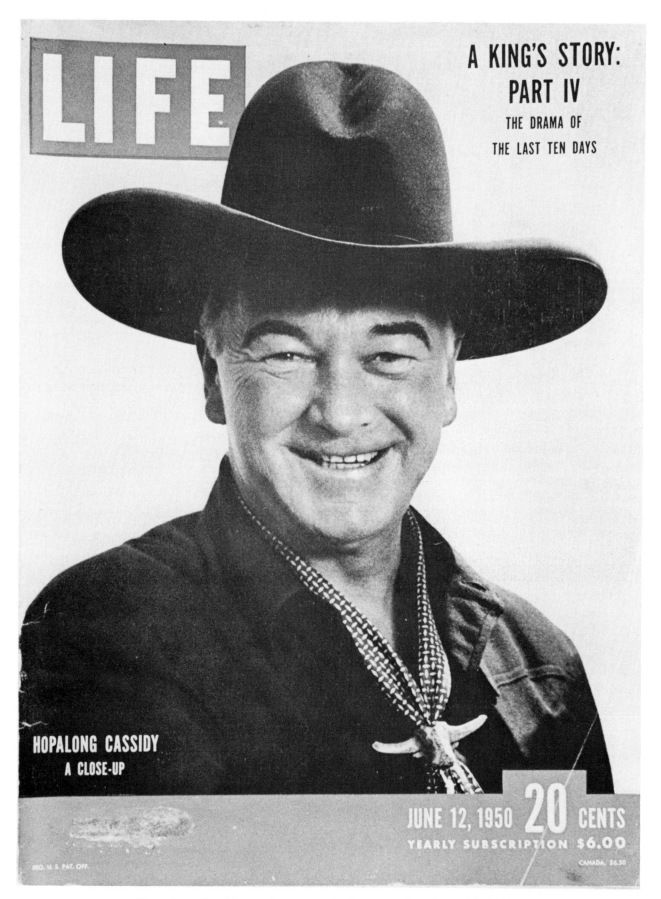

Hopalong Cassidy on the cover of Life *magazine, June 12, 1950.*

COWBOY IN BLACK

Wearing a black cowboy shirt, a black wide-brimmed Stetson, black britches, and shining black boots, Hopalong Cassidy, with his piercing steel-blue eyes and shock of silver-white hair, became the idol of millions of tots, first in his 1930s Western movies and later as the first cowboy of television.

Clarence E. Mulford first conceived of the fictitious character Hopalong Cassidy in 1905 in Brooklyn, New York. Mulford, formerly a marriage license clerk, had never seen the real West but had a good idea of what it was like, and he had once dreamed of being a cowboy himself. His first Western short story, called "The Fight at Buckskin," was sold to *Outing* magazine for $90, and the central story was incorporated into a first book called *Bar-20*. The handsome straight man (of what became a series of novels) was initially a stalwart cowhand named Buck Peters; but the author soon shifted his focus to Buck's "ornery," "cussin'," "tobacco-stained" sidekick, Hopalong Cassidy, who got the nickname—Hop-Along—because of his limp. A near-illiterate who spoke in a "git alongin'," "purty," "plum loco" Western jargon, this Hopalong was supposed to be somewhat on the side of the Good Guy of the West, but he always managed to kill off anywhere from two to thirteen redskins or whites per episode. While swigging corn whiskey as if it were water, he would shoot a man down and afterward would pause to "ventilate." A second or two later, he would pin down a black fly on a table with a stream of his brown tobacco spit.

For a number of years Mulford ground out this sort of pulp Western fiction until he had produced eighteen Hopalong volumes, including

Hopalong Cassidy
The Coming of Cassidy
Hopalong Cassidy Sees Red
Hopalong Cassidy's Private War

Hopalong Cassidy's Rustler Round-Up
Bar 20
Bar 20 Days
Buck Peters, Ranchman
Johnny Nelson
The Man from Bar 20

Originally published by A. C. McClurg & Company, and later in reprint by A. L. Burt and Grosset & Dunlap, these books sold well in England and America and were translated into several foreign languages, enabling the author, in the 1920s, to make his first trip to the West he so admired. However, this modest success with the fictional character Hopalong Cassidy would never have made the author the wealthy man he eventually became had it not been for a far-seeing junior partner at Doubleday, Doran, Mulford's later publisher, who in 1935 inserted the words "and television" into a contract with movie producer Harry "Pop" Sherman. Sherman wanted to produce "B" Westerns and regarded the TV clause as inconsequential. He had heard of reserving radio and other rights for an author—but television? Naturally Sherman signed the movie contract, and the rest is pop-culture cowboy history.

William Boyd, like so many others, came West in 1919 to find fame and fortune in Hollywood. Born in 1898 in Hendrysburg, Ohio, where his father was a poor farm laborer, young Bill quit school after the sixth grade to find work. After a youth of restless meandering and a variety of dull jobs, such as used-car salesman, lumberjack, grocery clerk, and menial work in a mining camp as well as in the Oklahoma oil fields, Boyd found employment with a car-hire chauffeur business in Los Angeles and married a wealthy heiress customer following their second ride around town. The marriage fizzled out quickly in the typical style of Tinseltown, but it managed to leave young and handsome William Boyd with a taste for the high life. Confident and aggressive, and with a new wardrobe to show for himself, Boyd wangled a job as an extra with Cecil B. DeMille. Befriended by the prestigious DeMille, Boyd in due time got larger roles in *King of Kings* and *Road to Yesterday,* later becoming a star of the silents in *The Volga Boatman, Two Arabian Nights,* and *Dress Parade.* These films made Boyd a romantic idol of the 1920s, in a class with such stars as Rod LaRocque and Wallace Reid. His salary jumped from $30 a week to $100,000 a year.

In the fabled manner of Hollywood of the 1920s, William Boyd spent his movie-made money as if there were no tomorrow, living lavishly, gambling fast, drinking heavily, and motoring all over town with jazz-baby starlets like Joan Crawford who loved to dance all night at parties and hot night spots. He bought a Beverly Hills mansion, a Malibu beach house, and a ranch; he married and divorced three actresses: Ruth Miller, Elinor Fair, and Dorothy Sebastian. A moralist or gossip-monger might view this helter-skelter situation as disaster-just-around-the-corner; the coincidence that tipped the proverbial scales might almost have been a device in a plot right out of the Hollywood Writers Dream Factory.

In 1931 Boyd, in pre-Hopalong western attire, was downing cowboy rotgut at a bar in a film called *The Painted Desert.* In that same year another actor with the name William Boyd, a saturnine heavy who had played Sergeant Quirk in *What Price Glory,* was having a drinking and gambling party at his ramshackle Hollywood abode when the police raided the place. Mistakenly, the newspapers featured a picture of the younger Boyd, the matinee idol who up until this incident had managed to suppress scandal in print. This error of identity cost the innocent Boyd his star status with the American public of the 1930s, ever on the lookout to bring down those idols who indulged in too much sin and vice. RKO promptly tore up his $300-a-week contract, telling him he was through in Hollywood. Four years later, "B" Western producer Harry "Pop" Sherman noted Boyd's down-and-out boozy predicament and saw an opportunity to get him cheaply for the role of the handsome Buck Peters in the *Hopalong* Western series he was preparing. Even though he was in out-of-luck circumstances, William Boyd told Harry Sherman he would only play the Hopalong character, stating his indifference to the

Felt Hopalong Cassidy pennant, c. 1950.

upright character of Buck Peters. Sherman reluctantly agreed to take a chance. He had a shock when on the first day's shooting Boyd confessed that he could not stay on a horse. A double was used until Boyd learned to ride, and later Cliff Lyons, a seasoned double for Ken Maynard and John Wayne, was employed to perform the difficult cowboy stunts.

It was a completely different Hopalong character that emerged in the Boyd-Sherman movies made over the next nine years. Only the first six pictures were remotely based on the original novels, and Boyd as Hopalong stopped "hopping" about after the very first film. The second film explained that the wounded leg had healed, and Boyd as Hoppy replaced the dirty shirts of the Mulford character with fancy black ones with white piping. He also gave up the chewing of cut plug and the random killing. Hopalong Cassidy now went about saving a widow's ranch from cattle rustlers and crooks out of the real inherent goodness of his cowboy soul. No longer a lazy cowpoke, he became a substantial, grammatical rancher who yearned to improve the community. Films usually ended with a fast-action chase in the final reel, but more often than not Hoppy did bring in the bad guys for justice without any killing. Rather than a glass of hard-earned Wild West whiskey, Hopalong would order a glass of sarsaparilla; and he was never known to kiss the heroine.

During the years he filmed the *Hopalong* series, Boyd himself underwent what some friends regarded as a major character change. Identifying with his role, he stopped smoking, drinking, and going to parties. In 1937 he met and married a beauteous blonde of twenty-three who had been a fan of his for ten years. She became his fifth wife, giving up her own stage and movie career to live quietly with Boyd on a ranch near Malibu, later moving with him

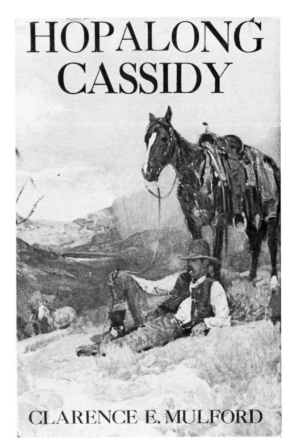

Hopalong Cassidy, *novel by Clarence E. Mulford published in Grosset & Dunlap series during the Depression.*

1920s autographed studio shot of silent screen star William Boyd inserted into a 1950s souvenir Hopalong Cassidy cardboard frame. Ted Hake collection.

Lobby card for United Artists film Mystery Man, *starring William Boyd, 1944. (P.C.)*

Hopalong Cassidy and the Stolen Treasure, *5″ x 5″ illustrated softcover published by Samuel Lowe Company, 1950. (P.C.)*

to a house in the Hollywood hills. Boyd said, "I never really was married before. The old Boyd no longer exists." Grace Bradley remained devoted to William Boyd until his death on September 12, 1972, from Parkinson's disease, congestive heart failure, and cancer.

Having signed Boyd for fifty-four pictures, Sherman stopped filming in 1943, but the star continued on his own, making twelve more of the Hopalong Cassidy movies and releasing them through United Artists. The transformed Boyd was out of work by the mid-1940s; he had such a strong identification with Hopalong that no one would hire him after his Western films lost appeal during the World War II years. Production costs were skyrocketing, and producers regarded the notion of Hopalong Cassidy films as outdated. But Boyd had a vision (or "tele-vision") of things to come. He even used television tricks in his last films, concentrating on close-ups and avoiding excessive long shots that he knew would be lost on a small TV set. He also instructed his writers and editors to schedule high points of action every twelve minutes for the possible inclusion of commercials.

Over several years, Boyd quietly made a series of television contracts with Mulford's publishers, with splits going from 25 to 50 percent. Gradually he rounded up the negatives from various owners of the Sherman pictures. A man with the unusual name of Toby Anguish initially handled the TV distribution, placing the first run of Hopalong films as sustaining programs on a Los Angeles station in 1948. They starred Boyd and his sidekick, George "Gabby" Hayes, Nora Lane, Russell Hayden, and others, with titles like *Hopalong Rides Again, Heart of Arizona, Hills of Old Wyoming, Texas Trail, Borderland, North of the Rio Grande, Trail Dust, Bar 20 Justice, Cassidy of Bar 20, Partners of the*

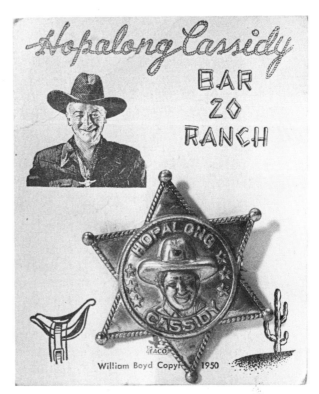

Hopalong Cassidy Bar 20 Ranch "Eaco" badge on original card, 1950.

Official Hopalong Cassidy pop-up birthday card by "Buzza" Cardozo, Hollywood.

Plains, and *Rustlers Valley.* Lesley Selander and Nate Watt were directors, and screenwriters were Norman Houston, Jack O'Donnell, and Al Martin. Boyd had spent $350,000 of his own cash and was dead broke; but he had been shrewd enough to corner the Hopalong Cassidy market for television.

In the late 1940s and early 1950s, kids who grew up during World War II were looking for a new hero, a real fighting man they could emulate. In war, as in every other walk of life, there are good guys and bad guys, and the children and adults of the time needed to believe that good guys always won out. Television had been around since the 1930s, but it was not commercially marketable until the late 1940s. Americans were awestruck when the little rectangular screen entered their living rooms,

showing nature films or travelogues. Something about William Boyd's Hopalong Cassidy image was perfect for the glowing little picture box. Perhaps it was the sharp black outfit against a white sky and gray terrain, or the man himself, who was old enough to be a father figure like Truman or Eisenhower. There was no doubt about it. Boyd, larger than life as Hoppy, corralled the children of America around their TV sets to watch the fast-action adventures of a cowboy who had never been a "real" cowboy himself, but who had learned to play his character to "reel" perfection. Three generations took to watching Hoppy adventures on TV—the grandparents who knew him as a DeMille matinee idol, parents who had watched Hopalong movies at theaters during the Depression, and the children of World War II.

Hopalong Cassidy collectibles: left to right: *16mm Castle Films tin lithographed lunch box manufactured by Aladdin Industries, dated 1954; plastic push-pull sparkler toy; ceramic mug, on top of Arvin radio; foreground, center:* "milk glass" *drinking glass. All 1950s.*

By 1950, once the cowboy in black was an established hit on TV, the selling of Hopalong Cassidy merchandise took the country by storm. Hoppy Trooper Clubs—with secret codes, cards, and pledges about being kind to birds and animals, and avoiding bad habits, and obeying your parents—became more popular than the Boy Scouts with the youngsters of America. Hopalong Cassidy Hitching Posts at major department stores featured Hoppy kiddie clothes with leather outfits selling for $45. Denim outfits sold from about $21 to $30, with the cheapest, a girl's outfit, selling for $4.95 ($1.95 extra for the hat). Boyd sold the Hoppy name to bread, candy bars, potato chips, puddings, cookies, peanut butter, toothpaste, hair creams, and other products—excepting bubble gum, which he detested. Clip-on Hoppy ties sold for 50 cents, four bars of soap with the Hoppy and Topper imprint were 59 cents, a wristwatch was $4.95 for the larger and $6.95 for the smaller, a trail knife was 98 cents, a pair of spur skates were $4.95, an animated nightlight was $3.95, and a two-gun Hoppy bicycle with handlebars in the shape of steer horns sold for $56.95. Hoppy toys, games, school supplies, books, and household items from dishware to wallpaper abounded, selling like hotcakes. Phonograph records and millions of comic books (which alone brought Boyd $60,000 annually) added to the Hoppy marketplace. Boyd said at one point, "I don't think there is any limit to what can be done," and declared that he had outmerchandised Mickey Mouse and that Gene Autry and Roy Rogers had dropped out of sight. Sportswear Hosiery marketed $165,000 worth of socks with the slogan "Hoppy Sox Make Happy Feet," and Gimbels placed an initial order for $22,500 worth of Hopalong Cassidy snowsuits. In 1950 Boyd's Hoppy character was doing 56 percent of all Western cowboy-hero business, with $70 million

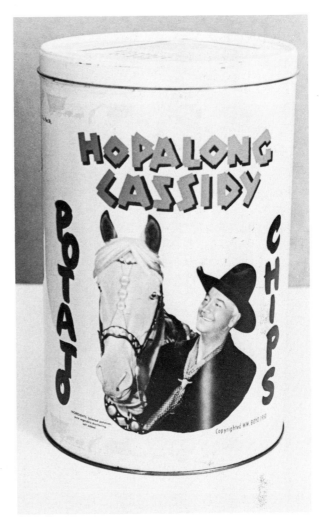

*Hopalong Cassidy Potato Chips, 1950.
Ted Hake collection.*

worth of merchandise sold annually, grossing Boyd $800,000 a year during his reign on TV. Boyd always insisted on high quality for his Hoppy goods, which is one reason Hoppy merchandise is sought after by those who favor cowboy collectibles today.

Hopalong Cassidy, a true twentieth-century Pied Piper character, also had kids tuning in to a radio show, which came on over Mutual in 1949, with Boyd himself as the voice of Hoppy and his sidekick, California, played by Andy Clyde. Eventually

Hoppy's Bar-20 Ranch Recipes, *White Star Tuna recipe booklet, c. 1950. Ted Hake collection. (T.H.)*

Hopalong Cassidy Hair Trainer, copyright William Boyd, 1950.

the show reached 500 stations and brought Boyd $50,000 a year. The Cole Brothers Circus, which was otherwise a slow-moving affair, broke all box-office records with Hopalong as its star. Boyd became one-third owner of the circus, which added to his already astronomical fortune. Personal appearances in department stores often found him shaking 50,000 hands. Hoppy loved children and always greeted them with the warm granddaddy-of-cowboys grin they expected. If Santa Claus shaved his beard and wore a black cowboy outfit, he would have probably become as popular as Hopalong Cassidy was to the children of the 1950s. At Gimbels in Philadelphia, Ellis Gimbel once asked of Boyd, "How do you do it?"

"They're my best friends—and your best customers," Boyd answered.

A story was circulated at the time about a mother who told her daughter that if she was good about getting over the measles, and if she prayed all year, Hoppy would come to see her on her birthday. The girl did exactly as her mother told her; she prayed and recovered. A desperate mother wrote to Hoppy explaining her predicament. Wouldn't he at least send a letter to her child on her upcoming birthday? Upset by the problem letter, Hoppy noted that the address was not far from where he would be on that date. Fitting the happy-birthday party into his busy schedule, he arrived in full regalia to find a group of children eating birthday cake on Hoppy paper plates on a Hoppy birthday table-cloth and with all the Hoppy party trim-mings—cards, favors, and napkins. When the mother began to weep, her daughter asked, "Why are you crying? I knew Hoppy was coming." Boyd was close to tears him-self but admonished the mother by saying, "You mustn't do this kind of thing if you don't believe in it." It was a Hoppy Birth-day for one little cowgirl.

With Hopalong Cassidy's indomitable belief in television as the new terrain of the Wild West, the other cowboys followed suit with their TV shows and merchandising ef-forts, notably the Lone Ranger, Gene Autry, and Roy Rogers, all with comic books, records, lunch boxes, and the rest.

By the end of the 1950s Hopalong Cas-sidy's fame was on the wane—but he had had a fantastic time of it. He had even been reunited with his old mentor, Cecil B. DeMille, in *The Greatest Show on Earth* (1952). There is a spectacular moment in the movie when he rides in on Topper with the circus—a cowboy in black on a white horse, in brilliant Technicolor. Actor Wil-liam Boyd will always be Hopalong Cassi-dy, a cowboy comet in the heaven of great western-style American heroes.

HOPALONG CASSIDY COLLECTIBLES

Hopalong Cassidy comics were published by Fawcett from 1943 to 1954. National

Periodical Publications picked up the pub-lication with issue #86 in February 1954 and continued through May–June 1959. *Master Comics,* published by Fawcett, is-sued Hopalong Cassidy stories in their an-thologies during the 1950s, and *Bill Boyd Western Comics* was issued, also, by Faw-cett from January 1950 to June 1952.

In 1950 Grape Nuts Flakes issued a give-away called *Hopalong Cassidy in "The Strange Legacy."* There were three Samuel Lowe Company storybooks published in 1950, about 48 pages long and measuring

Bond Bread cowboy giveaway premium card came in a series that described "Ways of the West" to youngsters.

5″ x 5″. Illustrated in color, the titles include *Stolen Treasure, Stagecoach,* and *Stampede.* In 1951 they issued *Hopalong Cassidy Gives a Helping Hand, His Friend Danny,* and *Little Tex.*

In 1950 Bonnie Book issued a hardcover book with a television screen on the cover, called *Hopalong Cassidy and His Young Friend Danny.* Grosset & Dunlap issued hardcover novels with dust jackets, including *The Coming of Cassidy* and *Hopalong Cassidy Sees Red.* Double D Westerns issued a hardcover novel with a dust jacket,

called *Hopalong Cassidy and the Trail to Seven Pines.*

Bonnie Book published two "hop-ups" (pop-ups) in 1950: *Hopalong Cassidy Lends a Helping Hand* and *Hopalong Cassidy and Lucky at the "Double-X" Ranch.* Lucky appeared in another 40-page, 9″ x 12″ book called *Hopalong and Lucky at the Bar Q* in 1950. Doubleday issued a hardcover novel in 1952 called *Hopalong Cassidy, Trouble Shooter.*

Hopalong Cassidy and the Two Young Cowboys was published by Cozy Corner

Hopalong Cassidy Happy Birthday card, c. 1950.

Books in 1950. Whitman issued a sticker-stencil-coloring book and a punch-out book called *Hopalong Cassidy Bar 20 Ranch* in 1951. Abbott Publishing put their *Hopalong Cassidy Coloring Book* on the market in 1950. Song sheets featuring Hoppy on the cover include "Where the Cimarron Flows" (1939), published by Famous Music Corporation, and "Take Me Back to Those Wide Open Spaces" (1936), published by Popular Melodies. Bond Bread was one of Hoppy's big sponsors and in addition to his autographed 8″ x 10″ color photo, you

could get the highly collectible Bond Bread end labels picturing Hoppy in various action deeds. These bread labels were numbered and were meant to be pasted in a hang-up album for the children's room. White Star Tuna issued a little booklet of "Hoppy's Bar-20 Ranch Recipes" so that you could have a great Bond Bread–White Star Tuna sandwich all officially approved by Hoppy. Capitol Records issued two 78-rpm double record albums with 20 pages of photos entitled *Hopalong Cassidy and the Singing Bandit* and *Hopalong Cassidy and*

Hopalong Cassidy Happy Birthday card, open.

Hopalong Cassidy doll, 21″ high with cloth body, leatherette belt, holster, and boots. Head is latex with painted features. Ted Hake collection.

the Square Dance Holdup. There is the Official Bar 20 TV Chair—a folding wooden chair, 22″ high with a red, black, and white canvas seat and back. The red metal Hoppy clothes hamper, with a Hoppy and Topper litho on the front, is a fine "usable" Hoppy collectible. There are at least four lamps, including the Bar 20 Ranch Lamp with a revolving color-action celluloid insert, a beige glass lamp with a color decal and shade, a beige glass gun-and-holster wall light with a color decal, and a beige glass light for the bedside.

To complete your Hoppy room in the 1950s you would have had Hoppy bedspreads and curtains, wallpaper, linoleum, a 24″ x 28″ throw rug, Hoppy's Bunkhouse Clothes Corral (a 24″-long wooden clothes rack offered by Garden Farm Milk), and an Official Hopalong Cassidy shoebag in red plastic with yellow and black pictures. Hoppy youngsters clamored for the playsuits, which included chaps, vest, shirt, neckerchief, and a holster and gun set. For inclement weather you could wear Hoppy rubber rainboots and Hoppy earmuffs. Leather products included the Hopalong Cassidy belt and Hopalong Cassidy wallet. There was also a plastic wallet with a color insert. Weco Products issued Dr. West's Dental Kit, which included a mirror with Hoppy's face outlined so that kids could actually *be* Hoppy, a black Hopalong toothbrush, and a tube of toothpaste with Hoppy's image repeated all over it. Associated Brands produced the Hopalong Cassidy Hair Trainer, issued both in handy "home" sizes and also in large bottles for barber shops. In 1950 Aladdin Industries produced a Hopalong Cassidy lunch box in red and blue and a thermos. Another school lunch kit was issued in 1954 with a fine tin-litho action graphic. There is a complete set of white chinaware with color imprints of Hoppy and Topper, including a 10″ plate, bowls, and mugs. There are three

Figure and paint set containing plaster figurines of Hoppy, Lucky, and California, Laurel Ann Arts, Los Angeles, Calif., 1950.

Dr. West's Hopalong Cassidy Dental Kit contains toothpaste, toothpaste box, toothbrush, glass toothbrush container, and mirror; original box.

Hopalong Cassidy earmuffs. Ted Hake collection.

different "milk-glass" mugs and three varieties of "milk-glass" juice and milk glasses. To complete your breakfast experience, a plastic placemat with Hoppy illustrations was available. And at the end of the day, you could climb into your Hoppy pajamas and wash your face with Hoppy and Topper soap.

Hopalong Cassidy made sure that there were plenty of games available to pass the rainy afternoons indoors. Milton Bradley came up with a board game in 1950 with metal figures of Hoppy on Topper and lots of Hoppy money to gamble with. The Hopalong Cassidy Western Frontier Set is an excellent boxed set with heavy cardboard punch-outs consisting of three-dimensional figures of Hoppy, cowboys, Indians, western buildings, and a stagecoach. Bradley issued this in addition to the Hopalong Cassidy Western Style Dominoes and the Hopalong Cassidy Chinese Checkers game. For more artistically inclined children, Laurel Ann Arts produced a figure and

Left: *The Official Galter Productions Hopalong Cassidy box camera with original box, 1940. Copyright William Boyd. (P.C.) Below: Authentic Hopalong Cassidy Western belt manufactured by Yale Belt Corp.*

paint set with white plaster figures of Hoppy, California, and Lucky. Stroehmann's Sunbeam Bread issued a handsome Hopalong Cassidy Ranch House Race game that instructed boys and girls to "tell Mom to buy Stroehmann's Sunbeam—it's Hoppy's favorite bread!" Southwest Traders issued the Hopalong Cassidy Bar 20 Chuckwagon Garden and Topper's Magic Green Pasture in 1950, which included a feedbag for Topper, a ranch press-out set, growing mats, and seeds. Ideal issued 6″-high plastic figures of Hoppy and Topper in a boxed set, and there is an excellent Hoppy doll, 21″ high with a cloth body, simulated leather belt, holster, and boots, a latex head with painted features, and a cloth hat and metal steer-head neckerchief slide. Pacific Playing Card Company included a Hoppy's Saddle canasta set in a revolving canasta tray with two decks of Hoppy cards and an official score pad. Joe Fredriksson Toy and Game Company's Hoppy money, called "Lucky Bucks," flooded the market. There was a boxed set of three Hopalong Cassidy puzzles.

Marx issued a Hopalong Cassidy Target Game, a beautiful litho on metal, and a fine tin wind-up with moving arm and lariat— another highly collectible piece. The Hopalong Cassidy Mechanical Shooting Gallery put out by the Automatic Toy Company is also a good tin. Auto-Magic had a Hopalong Cassidy Picture Gun and Theater, with a gun and seven films. For younger kids a plastic sparkler-type gun and a red plastic Hoppy "Zoomerang" gun, which shot paper rolls, were available. The Official Hopalong Cassidy Pistol and Spurs set, which includes a pearl-handled metal .44 pistol triggered to fire real caps, two silver spurs with chains, and two fancy spur "leathers," was for more advanced Hoppy enthusiasts. America's "favorite Western star" has his likeness and autograph on the pearl handle and appears astride Topper

Hopalong Cassidy's Target Game, 15″ x 27″ tin litho, manufactured by Marx, c. 1950.

on the handsome box. The Buck'n Bronc gun, which features a black pearl handle with a white pearl likeness of Hopalong superimposed, was offered as a holstered set of two accompanying the Rollfast Hopa-

long Cassidy bicycle, which also featured genuine leather holsters, Western studded guards, horsehair-grained saddle, longhorn handlebars, and a frontier-fringed carrier. The Shoot with Hoppy Official Hopalong

Cardboard advertisement for Rollfast Hopalong Cassidy Bicycle. Courtesy Jim Miller, of Renninger's #1, Indoor Antique Market, Adamstown, Pa.

Hopalong Cassidy "Buck'n Bronc" six-shooter cap pistol. This handsome gun was in a holstered set and came with the Hopalong Cassidy Rollfast Bicycle. Courtesy Jim Miller, of Renninger's #1, Indoor Antique Market, Adamstown, Pa.

The Hopalong Cassidy Rollfast Bicycle, complete with two-gun holster set, fringed carrier, white-wall balloon tires, and embossed metal Hoppy insignia, 1950s. Courtesy Jim Miller, of Renninger's #1, Indoor Antique Market, Adamstown, Pa.

Cassidy #120 Box Camera was offered in a well-designed box, and you could get a flash attachment decorated with striking black-and-white photos of Hoppy on Topper. And Arvin produced a Hopalong Cassidy metal table radio painted in red or black with silver trim. There is a Hoppy Statuette Bank in brown plastic, a drum and drumstick made by Rubbertone, field glasses with decals, pencil cases, ballpoint pens, writing paper, a leather-bound scrapbook with an embossed picture, leather wrist guards, greeting cards, sets of postcards issued in conjunction with Hoppy's movies, collectible Post Cereal cards in sets of thirty-six, jewelry by Anson, including tie bars and key-ring chains, and Hopalong Cassidy Bar-20 Ranch "Eaco" metal pins, barrettes, and badges. There is also a Hopalong Cassidy Bar-20 metal money clip with a polarizing lens. Various pinback buttons in celluloid and lithographed tin were issued by companies like the *Daily News,* which carried the Hoppy funnies daily and Sunday, and Dairylea Milk, which claimed it was Hoppy's favorite. Hoppy's watches and clocks were made by the U.S. Time Corporation from 1950 well into the late 1960s and were handsomely boxed. They include a pocket watch, a wristwatch, and an alarm clock. Hoppy sent a personal-improvement note with each timepiece:

Hi Pardner!

Time is the most important thing in your lives. Even one minute wasted is a moment lost that could have been spent in helping you to be a better and happier person. Since time is important to you it is just as important to other people. Wrong as it is to waste your own time, it is even worse to waste the time of your friends. Be prompt and punctual with your appointments . . . I sincerely hope that this watch will be a means of bringing you great joy, happiness and success by keeping track of every minute of every hour of your most important TIME. Good Luck. Hoppy.

Hopalong Cassidy pinback button collectibles; Dairylea, Hoppy's favorite milk; Hopalong Cassidy in the Daily News; *Hopalong "official" rodeo handout and souvenir button, manufactured in both green and red. All 1950s.*

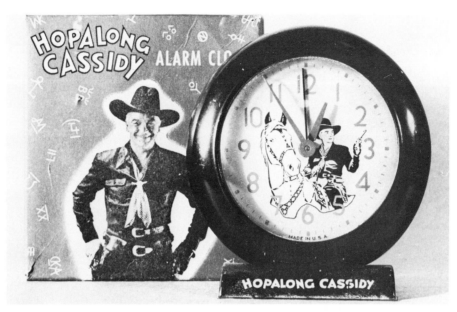

Hopalong Cassidy Alarm Clock with original box,
U.S. Time Co., 1950. Robert Lesser collection. (P.C.)

Hopalong Cassidy wristwatch, U.S. Time Co.,
1950. Robert Lesser collection.

Hopalong Cassidy wristwatch cardboard box.
Robert Lesser collection.

COWBOY–COWGIRL ROUNDUP

Hollywood divided its Western film production into two categories—"A" for the top of the line and "B" for those on a "cheapie" budget. Western "Bs," sometimes referred to as horse operas, were ground out like so much celluloid pulp to fill in double or triple features during the Depression and World War II years. According to Hollywood formula there were seven or eight basic "B" plots, usually centered on a cow town where the bad guys hung out drinking and gambling, an honest ranchman and his daughter who were constantly besieged by cattle rustlers or land-hungry sharpshooters, and a sheriff hero who with his posse of cowboy good guys would resolve the age-old problem of good guys vs. bad.

More essential than plot or quick-draw action was the cowboy star himself; and if an attractive cowgirl or rancher's daughter or a widowed schoolteacher was thrown in as part of a subplot, so much the better. Movie images were larger than life, and a star had to impress an audience with presence of personality as well as good looks. Costume played an important part; the hero's cowboy outfit became more and more elaborate, including fancy silk-fringe shirts, tight-fitting pants, boots with spurs, and big hats. At the top of this genre were Tom Mix, Hopalong Cassidy, and the singing cowboys Roy and Gene. Chases, stunts, fistfights, and fast-gun draw were essential. A cowboy star sometimes found himself forever typecast, going from one Western production to another, sometimes making two or three at the same time. This type of movie schedule demanded a strong constitution, which is why so many cowboy stars at one time or other were real cowboys. "Reel" cowboys performed real stunts on their horses, and in the public's mind they became as real as those who originally rode the early cattle trails.

Charles "The Durango Kid" Starrett was typical of this breed. Educated in the East, this handsome actor went to Hollywood to make dozens of "B" films with titles like *West of Abilene* and *The Masked Stranger.* Johnny Mack Brown, who began in the silents in the 1920s, was coached in drawing a gun and mounting a horse by William S. Hart for the early sound film *Billy the Kid,* after which he embarked on twenty years of working exclusively on Westerns for the chief "B" studios—Supreme, Republic, Universal, Monogram, and Allied Artists. Johnny Mack Brown appeared in a film as recently as 1966—*Apache Uprising.* Guy Madison, who began as the glamour-guy sailor the bobby-soxers adored in Selznick's *Since You Went Away* in the early 1940s, went on to make a number of Westerns such as *The Yellow-Haired Kid, Six-Gun Decision,* and *Massacre River.* He became well known as a Western hero when he made a TV series, *Wild Bill Hickok,* which was very popular with kids in the early 1950s. A major TV merchandising effort was associated with this series, including box-top premiums, picture puzzles, toy guns, and other items that are among today's cowboy collectibles. Chuck Connors and John Payne also were popular on TV, and later James Garner in *Maverick* would dominate the Western television terrain, not unlike Larry Hagman in the recent *Dallas* TV series.

Lash LaRue, a poor man's Humphrey Bogart, wore an all-black cowboy outfit and carried a bullwhip in a series of Westerns with titles like *Cheyenne Takes Over, King of the Bull Whip,* and *Thundering Trail.* LaRue was a former hairdresser who never seemed at home in the saddle and

Built-Rite Junior Picture Puzzle featuring Guy Madison as Wild Bill Hickok sold for 29 cents in 1956.

who horsed around with an emaciated, pint-sized sidekick à la Gabby Hayes named Al "Fuzzy" St. John, who originally had been a Keystone Kop. Lash's low-budget films of the early 1950s, produced by Ron Ormond's Western Adventure Productions, were popular in a perverse sort of way with those who looked for a more sinister, sadistic bent in their cowboy hero. Lash LaRue became a kind of "camp" cowboy, a real novelty in the sometimes overly serious 1950s. He gained many fans on early TV, but his cowboy career was short-lived. A religious fanatic at one point, LaRue later hit the skids with booze in the manner of an old Hollywood cowboy tradition.

Other popular cowboy stars include "Wild Bill" Elliott, George O'Brien, Gordon Elliott, Tom Tyler, Bob Steele, Bill Cody, Tim McCoy, Rex Bell, Tom Keene, Jack Hoxie, Harry Carey, Fess Parker, Sunset Carson, Allan Lane, Rod Cameron,

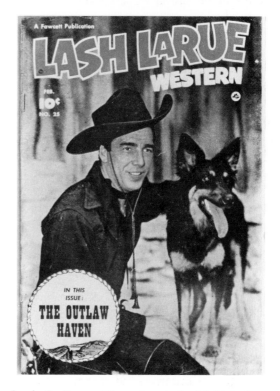

Lash LaRue with a dog pal sidekick in a Fawcett comic book, February 1952. Ted Hake Collection. (T.H.)

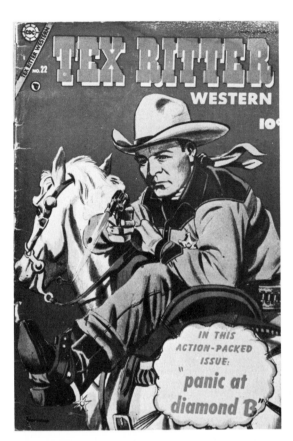

Top left: Gabby Hayes Western Cowboy Comic, *Fawcett, May 1950. Hayes typifies the cowboy star's comedy-relief sidekick; he appeared in supportive roles opposite Roy Rogers, William Boyd, and others. (P.C.)* Above: Tex Ritter Western *comic book, published by Charlton Comics Group, May 1954.* Left: Wild Bill Elliott Comics, *Dell, 1954. (P.C.)*

Wally Wales, George Montgomery, Bob Nolan, Lane Chandler, Tim Holt, Bob Livingston, Whip Wilson, Buster Crabbe, and the previously mentioned Buck Jones, Fred Thomson, Hoot Gibson, and Ken Maynard. In the 1930s and 1940s over thirty Western stars were galloping away, making as many as eight movies per year each. Famous "B" Western cowboy sidekicks were Andy Devine, George "Gabby" Hayes, Andy Clyde, Fuzzy Knight, Smiley Burnette, Chill Wills, Yakima Canutt, Henry Hull, and Frank Ferguson. "B" Western singing cowboys included Tex Ritter—whose recording hits were "You Two-Timed Me One Time Too Often," "Blood on the Saddle," "Cielito Lindo," "Jingle, Jangle, Jingle," and "The Old Chisholm Trail"—Bob Baker, Fred Scott, Jack Randall, Monte Hale, Jimmy Wakeley (another popular country-and-western recording artist), Eddie Dean, and Rex Allen, who has been called the last of the singing cowboys. Dick Foran, Warner Brothers' only singing cowboy, had a better than average singing voice, closer to Nelson Eddy's than to Gene Autry's, and he was a much better actor than Autry. His film *Moonlight on the Prairie* was made only two months after the release of Autry's *Tumbling Tumbleweeds*, in September 1935. His Westerns, including *Treachery Rides the Range*, *Song of the Saddle*, *California Mail*, *Cherokee Strip*, *Empty Holsters*, and *Prairie Thunder*, always had high production standards and action content that remained central to the plot. The songs entered into the scenario easily and naturally, never becoming overblown productions as in the Autry series. Foran made twelve Westerns from 1935 to 1937 before going on to success as a straight actor for Warner's.

An actor who established himself as a first-rate performer above and beyond his cowboy abilities became an "A" cowboy, which meant that his movies were given top production attention and top promotion by a major studio. Such a cowboy actor was John "Duke" Wayne, who epitomizes to many fans today the cowboy hero of all time. Born Marion Michael Morrison on May 26, 1907, in Winterset, Iowa, he first became an extra in *Mother Machree* in 1928. During the filming of this picture John Ford took a liking to the rugged, handsome actor and gave him work in *Hangman's House* (1928), *Salute* (1929), and *Men Without Women* (1930). His first

Sheet music: "My Little Buckaroo," from the Warner Bros. Western musical Cherokee Strip, *starring Dick Foran, the Singing Cowboy, published by M. Whitmark & Sons, 1937. Mary Evans collection.*

John "Duke" Wayne glossy studio postcard sendaway, c. 1940.

A rare cardboard color litho lobby poster from the first film to star a young John Wayne, an epic "all talking" Fox Western, The Big Trail, *1930. From the collection of Leonard L. Lasko.*

starring role was in Raoul Walsh's 70mm big-screen, $2 million Western *The Big Trail*. Movie theaters in 1930 had to buy special equipment to show this landmark film, and because the Depression was hitting hard it became economically unfeasible. Wayne then went into a series of Westerns, including some with Buck Jones and Tim McCoy as the stars. Not until *Stagecoach* in 1939 did he emerge out of the "B" cowboy category. *Stagecoach* became a classic Western; and other top-notch Wayne Westerns include *Red River, Tall in the Saddle,* and *True Grit,* for which he won an Academy Award in 1970. Wayne's last film, *Rooster Cogburn and the Lady* (1975), co-starring Katherine Hepburn, was a Western also. In all, the Duke made over 150 films; a number of them, of course, were "B" Westerns from Universal, Republic, Columbia, or Monogram, with titles like *King of the Pecos, The Oregon Trail, The Lonely Trail, Ride 'Em Cowboy, The Big Stampede, Range Feud, Lawless Frontier, Lucky Texan, 'Neath Arizona Skies, Red River Range,* and *Sagebrush Trail.* A few college-football flicks are in there, and in the 1940s it was World War II in *Back to Bataan.* Westerns were always a favorite of John Wayne's, and he is strongly identified as a red-white-and-blue cowboy American. Although he established himself as a fighting man in *She Wore a Yellow Ribbon, The Green Berets,* and *Sands of Iwo Jima,* most fans prefer to think of him as Big Jim McLain, alias Cowboy John, the ideal man of the West who came out of Hollywood.

Gary Cooper is another "A" Western cowboy actor deluxe, notably in *The Plainsman* (in which he played Wild Bill Hickok), *The Westerner, The Virginian, The Cowboy and the Lady, Man of the West, Hanging Tree,* and *The Texan.* One of the great Westerns of all time was *High Noon* (1952), with Gary Cooper impeccable as an older lawman who nearly loses his

self-respect in a corrupt cow town. A young Grace Kelly was the girl, and Tex Ritter sang the theme song. Gary Cooper began as an extra in silent Westerns in 1925, *The Thundering Herd* and *The Lucky Horseman* among them. He is always associated with the lean-and-lanky-tall-in-the-saddle-handsome-cowboy type, with underlying sexual tension just about to break loose. His style was indirect and underplayed, as opposed to John Wayne's macho eyeball-to-eyeball directness. Wayne was idealized as a man's man; the Cooper image set the ladies' hearts aflutter with his boyish grin and sulking charm.

Many major stars began in Westerns or at one point in their career kicked the dust in an "A" or "B" giddy-apper. One of Clark Gable's first movies was a cowboy epic called *The Painted Desert* (1930), in which he played a villain in conflict with a pre-Hopalong William Boyd. Other Gable Westerns include *Honky Tonk* with Lana Turner, *Across the Wide Missouri, Lone Star, The King and Four Queens,* and *The Misfits,* a modern Western written by Arthur Miller for his wife Marilyn Monroe and also starring Montgomery Clift. Clift was notable in *Red River,* and Marilyn Monroe gave an electric performance in *The River of No Return,* with Robert Mitchum and Rory Calhoun. Joan Crawford appeared in *Law of the Range* and a Western musical called *Montana Moon.* Rita Hayworth served her time in "B" Westerns such as *Trouble in Texas* (1937) with singing cowboy Tex Ritter, and *The Renegade Ranger* with Tim Holt and Ray Whitley. (Ray Whitley coauthored Gene Autry's theme song, "Back in the Saddle Again.") Marlene Dietrich's career was given a boost by her performance as Frenchy in the 1939 classic *Destry Rides Again,* based on Max Brand's novel and co-starring Jimmy Stewart. Her other Western follow-ups include

The Spoilers (1942) and *Rancho Notorious* (1952). Henry Fonda gave a fine performance as Frank James in *Jesse James,* repeating this role in *The Return of Jesse James.* He also played Wyatt Earp in *My Darling Clementine* and continued with Westerns in *Fort Apache, The Tin Star,* and *Warlock.* Randolph Scott starred in a series of Zane Grey adaptations in the 1930s, and after 1947 made Westerns exclusively. Many of the ones he co-produced with Harry Joe Brown were in the "A" category. Scott was one of the foremost actors to appear in a great number of Westerns,

as was Joel McCrea, who played Buffalo Bill, Sam Houston, Wyatt Earp, Bat Masterson, and other Western characters in a long list of Hollywood films. In 1974 McCrea narrated a film called *The Great American Cowboy,* a subject that had become very much a part of McCrea. Both Randolph Scott and Joel McCrea had a soft, solid, strong-yet-passive shy quality that came across with a truly American cowboy flavor—not unlike Henry Fonda or Gary Cooper.

One Western actor who should be given special note here is Ronald Reagan, who

Ronald Reagan must have learned a great deal about fighting for "law and order" in Western films such as this one made in 1953. Large-size original presidential cum Western movie posters have become scarce collectors' items.

Wearing the pants and toting a gun, Joan Crawford seems completely in control as a saloon keeper in Johnny Guitar, *1954, in this "on a Hollywood set" movie publicity still.*

has brought his soft-spoken cowboy touch into the White House.* Reagan made a number of films before moving into politics and California ranch life; the Western ones are *Cowboy from Brooklyn* (1938), in which Pat O'Brien is a cowboy and Reagan is the straight man, *The Santa Fe Trail* (1940), in which Reagan plays Custer, *The Bad Man* (1941), *The Last Outpost* (1951), *Law and Order* (1953), *Cattle Queen of Montana* (1954), and *Tennessee's Partner* (1955). Reagan played host in 1964 on the Western TV series *Death Valley Days,* an offshoot of the famous radio show. A commercial Reagan did for 20 Mule Team Borax had housewives writing in saying that not only would they buy Borax from "Ronnie" but they would vote for him for President. The rest is history. Other than in his role as President, it is generally acknowledged that Ronald Reagan's best performance was in a non-Western for Warner's, *Kings Row,* opposite Ann Sheridan, although his most famous one may now be *Bedtime for Bonzo,* in which he ape-sits for a monkey. The Ronald Reagan–Nancy Davis lifestyle, it has been said, was influenced by another Hollywood Western couple—Roy Rogers and Dale Evans.

*Ronald Reagan is himself a real cowboy buff, not only spending his spare time horseback riding and working his ranch but avidly collecting western art and historical prints, spurs, and saddles, as well as cowboy memorabilia.

Many actresses played sidekick cowgirls, most notably Dale Evans, Penny Edwards, Noreen Nash, Kay Buckley, Reno Browne, Estelita, Jane Frazee, Mary Beth Hughes (a Marilyn Monroe–Lana Turner look-alike), Barbara Britton, Peggy Castle, Rhonda Fleming, Ellen Drew, Marie Windsor (usually a saloon-girl temptress), Evelyn Finley, Evelyn Young, Catherine McLeod, Jean Dixon, Gail Davis, Ruth Mix, Jane Bryan, Evelyn Brent, and Nan Leslie. Usually women who were in Westerns were billed below the cowboy star and were regarded by the studios as starlets. This chauvinism continued in most Western films right up through *Butch Cassidy and the Sundance Kid,* except when a major female star such as Barbara Stanwyck or Joan Crawford decided to go Western. Stanwyck portrayed some memorable Western heroines, who were usually hard as nails and as tough as any man. Notable among Stanwyck's Western features were *Annie Oakley, Cattle Queen of Montana, The Maverick Queen,* and *California.* Joan Crawford followed suit with an incredibly tough lady-who-wore-the-pants performance in *Johnny Guitar,* which pitted her against an equally vicious Mercedes McCambridge. The on-screen battle between these two cowgirls made headlines when they continued their fight off-screen as well. Sterling Hayden, a top-notch actor, had to play second fiddle to these two hard-boiled dames. One *Films in Review* critic coined the term "post-menopause virility" to describe the volatile Joan Crawford.

Heavy-duty sensuality came into the Western when Jane Russell as Rio contemplated seducing Billy the Kid (Jack Beutel) in the Howard Hughes production of *The Outlaw* in 1943. *Duel in the Sun* followed in 1945, with Gregory Peck as a lecherous cowboy chasing after an enticing Jennifer Jones. *Duel in the Sun* was referred to tongue-in-cheek by film critics as *Lust in the Dust.* Both films had a field day with the censors. They helped to form a new marketplace for sexy Western paperbacks in the 1940s, '50s, and '60s.

Hollywood and Broadway produced many big Western-style musical fantasies that created cowboy-cowgirl trends. An *Annie Get Your Gun* on Broadway, starring Ethel Merman with blue-black hair, wound up as a super-colossal M-G-M movie starring blond bombshell Betty Hutton, both portraying the energetic Annie Oakley, who had been billed in Buffalo Bill's Wild West Show "Little Sure Shot, a Wonder of the Age." In 1928 Ziegfeld offered a stunning Broadway musical spectacle called *Whoopee* as a vehicle for Eddie Cantor and also starring Ruth Etting, Ethel Shutta, and Tamara Geva. The sets, and in particular the incredible cowboy, cowgirl, and Indian costumes, all with a Western Deco motif, created a sensation. Cantor re-created this show in 1929 in a Technicolor sound film, which holds up remarkably well by today's standards. This film is also an opportunity for stage buffs to study an almost perfect rendition of a Ziegfeld stage show. *Girl Crazy,* the George Gershwin Broadway musical that featured Ethel Merman and Ginger Rogers, became another Western musical film extravaganza in 1943 with Judy Garland and Mickey Rooney; Busby Berkeley created the whip-cracking dance sequences. This movie musical is one of M-G-M's best. "Bidin' My Time," with Judy and a chorus of cowboys, is a show-stopper. Other Broadway musicals with a strong Western theme would include *Oklahoma!,* by Rodgers and Hammerstein, which also made a successful transition to Hollywood. In the 1930s Jeanette MacDonald and Nelson Eddy starred in two M-G-M musicals with a Western operetta setting: *The Girl of the Golden West* and *Rose-*

Slot-machine penny postcards of 1940s and 1950s movie cowgirls came in sets of 32 and were usually printed in blue, sepia, or green. Top row, left to right: Jacqueline White, Teddi Sherman, Kay Buckley. Second row: Jane Frazee, Penny Edwards, Estelita. Third row: Reno Browne, Noreen Nash, Mona Freeman.

Ethel Merman in fancy "flash cowgirl" garb as Annie Oakley on the cover of a 78-rpm collectible album of Annie Get Your Gun, *with music and lyrics by Irving Berlin, from the Rodgers and Hammerstein Broadway production. Six-record set, Decca, 1946.*

Decorative Western-style sheet music featuring Eddie Cantor in the early Technicolor film Whoopee, *published by Donaldson, Douglas & Gumble. (P.C.)*

Marie, which was made again in the 1950s with Ann Blyth. Western movie and stage musicals were usually highly stylized and were meant to be very American in spirit and song. The songs were less thoroughly Western than those in the singing-cowboy movies. Gershwin, Rodgers and Hammerstein, Gus Kahn, and Irving Berlin were, to be sure, big-city sophisticates, and this quality as well as the particular genius of each entered into the music and the productions.

The east coast equivalent of Hollywood's Hitching Post Theatre was the New York Theatre in Time Square. For many years horse opera double bills were shown, featuring all the top cowboy stars, to the delight of adults and kids who loved the fast-action chases between good guys and bad guys. In 1953 the New York Theatre stopped showing Westerns in favor of Italian art films. The last cowboy movie shown there was also the last one Gene Autry made for Columbia, called *The Last of the Pony Riders,* with his sidekick Smiley Burnette.

ROUNDUP COLLECTIBLES

Cowboy collectibles from "A" and "B" films would certainly include the movie posters themselves, lobby cards, 8″ x 10″ stills, and penny-arcade postcards of cowboy or cowgirl stars. Posters and lobby cards are very attractive when framed, and many of these are to be found in movie specialty shops, antique shops, auctions, and print shops or at the special movie-memorabilia shows, which usually take place in hotels and are advertised in advance in trade and local daily newspapers. Western posters and lobby cards are on the

way to becoming classic American collectibles; collectors often go about their search for a particular favorite as if they were searching for some archaeological treasure. The actual Wild West existed only about a hundred years back, while the golden age of popular western culture was just forty or fifty years ago. No matter. Time concepts seemed to change radically in the mid-1960s, when everyone grasped that the age of the cheap disposable was really here to stay (Andy Warhol, pop artist supreme, called it "the Plastic Inevitable"). People feverishly began to collect whatever came from prior decades, and collectibles began to appear right next to more bona fide antiques, be they a Mickey Mouse bisque toothbrush holder, a Log Cabin Syrup tin, a Planter's Peanuts jar, or a Hopalong Cassidy lunch box.

From the TV era many cowboy collect-

Whoopee *cowboy car, litho on tin wind-up revolving action toy, manufactured by Marx, c. 1930.*

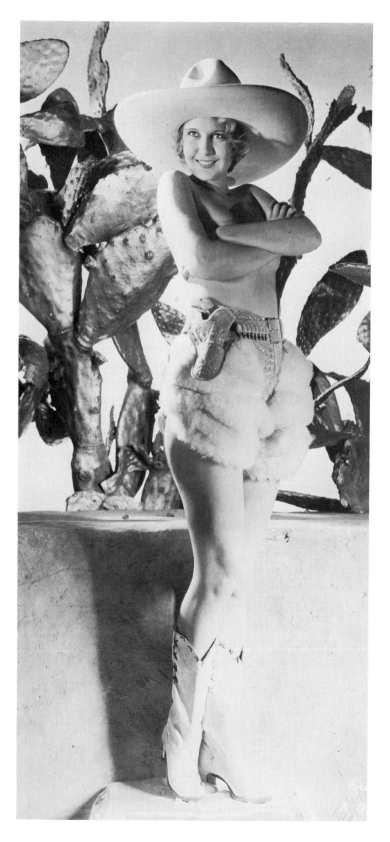

Movie starlet in risqué cowgirl attire for a promotional 8″ x 10″ still from the Ziegfeld-Goldwyn movie Whoopee, *United Artists, 1929.*

Right: *Mickey Rooney and Judy Garland as cowboy-cowgirl pals in the 1943 M-G-M movie* Girl Crazy, *from an M-G-M promotional campaign book. Dr. Leo's "Vitamin 12" refers to twelve "pep-up" movies released at that time.*

Sheet music from Rhythm on the Range, *a Paramount Western musical starring cowpoke songster Bing Crosby and a beautiful blond Frances Farmer, published by Famous Music Corp., 1936.*

ibles center on Guy Madison's *Wild Bill Hickok* show for Sugar Pops, including a Junior Picture Puzzle from 1956 and a Wild Bill Hickok and Jingles (Andy Devine) Official Diamond Cowboy Outfit with a genuine leather holster set with two guns. *Gunsmoke* merchandise includes a Marshal Matt Dillon (played by James Arness) holster set and an authorized Big Little Book put out by Whitman in their new TV series

NO BUSINESS LIKE SHOW BUSINESS

in 1958. In 1967 Whitman issued a Big Little Book for *Bonanza*, the longest-running TV show, called *The Bubble Gum Kid*. Aladdin Industries manufactured a nice raised-tin-litho lunch box; Dell/Gold Key issued comics for *Bonanza, Gunsmoke,* and *Wagon Train*. Also from *Wagon Train* came a handsome hand-tooled leather holster set with two six-guns.

Comic books from this era feature John Wayne, Lash LaRue, Johnny Mack Brown,

Sunset Carson, Wild Bill Elliott, Monte Hale, Allan "Rocky" Lane, Tex Ritter, Rex Hart, Rex Allen, Bob Steele, Whip Wilson, and others.

Distance allows us to notice changes in graphics, style, and paper quality from the silent era to the 1950s. Generally, the earlier the decade, the higher the prices. Lately even items from the fifties and sixties are becoming scarce—but then these decades

Tim Holt penny-arcade slot-machine postcard, 1940s.

Gunsmoke, *a Big Little Book, featuring James Arness as Matt Dillon from the CBS TV program, Whitman, 1958. (P.C.)*

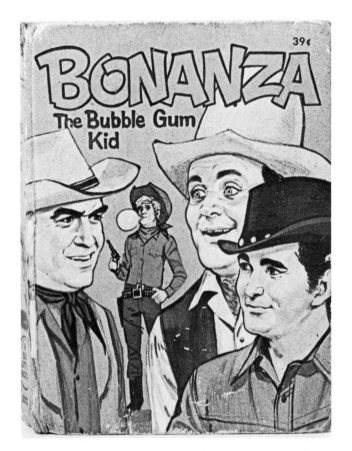

were a long time ago to some. One reason for the increasing demand for things western, or Cowboy Collectibles, is the new interest in a dominant American cultural theme, the Wild West. So now even Hoppy, Roy, Gene, and Tom are an integral part of the new modern Western lifestyle. Galloping fast after them are the "B's" and some of those gone-but-not-forgotten TV cowboys. Catch them while you can!

Bonanza: *"The Bubble Gum Kid," a Big Little Book by George S. Elrick, from the NBC TV show, Whitman, 1967.*

Bonanza: *Litho on metal "round-up" school lunch box from Aladdin Industries, c. 1960s.*

COWBOY DOODY

Hopalong Cassidy's chief cowboy competitor for TV audiences in the late 1940s and the 1950s was a red-haired freckle-faced, blue-eyed, grinning, toothy, wooden-headed puppet named Howdy Doody, created by a "network cowboy" hustler named Buffalo Bob Smith. Just as a sophisticated wooden dummy wearing a tuxedo and a monocle had been the rage with radio listeners on the Chase and Sanborn Hour (*The Edgar Bergen and Charlie McCarthy Show*) in the 1930s and 1940s, Howdy Doody now had children glued to their television screen, watching what probably still holds the record as the most looked-at kiddie TV show of all time.

Howdy Doody became an important aspect of the cowboy craze when he first appeared on NBC-TV on December 27, 1947. His show and the merchandising of Howdy Doody products galloped after Hoppy and Topper in popularity. A line of Howdy Doody puppet marionette dolls also included the other favorites on the show: Clarabel the Clown, Princess Summer-Fall-Winter-Spring, Dilly Dally, and Mr. Bluster. Among the many merchandising items that are collectibles of today are metal tin-litho lunch boxes, lamps, coloring books, song books, tin-litho wind-up toys, cookie jars, banks, hats, Howdy Doody guitars, watches, Howdy Doody masks, clothing, storybooks, comic books, and records. The Howdy (and friends) image was imprinted on the Welch's grape jelly glasses, ice-cream pops, Royal Gelatin Desserts (Howdy Doody's favorite), shoe polish, and countless other edibles and usables. The *Howdy Doody Show* was sponsored by various companies, including Colgate Dental Cream, which had Howdy singing, "You know it's right if it's red and white," referring to the packaging colors.

HOWDY DOODY, THE SINGING COWBOY

Music Is Fun with Howdy Doody, *illustrated songbook published by Children's Songs, Inc., 1949. Copyright Bob Smith. (P.C.)*

Four-inch plastic figure of Howdy Doody, singing cowboy, at the NBC microphone, 1950. Copyright Bob Smith. (P.C.)

Howdy Doody puppet, painted composition with flannel shirt, neckerchief, and vinyl boot tops. Copyright Bob Smith. Fred Orlansky collection.

Princess Summer-Fall-Winter-Spring, painted composition with flannel "buckskin" outfit. Copyright Bob Smith. Fred Orlansky collection.

Ovaltine offered a handsome red plastic shake-up mug with a blue top that had a decal on it of Howdy spouting, "Howdy Doody...be keen...be keen...Drink chocolate flavored Ovaltine." A similar Ovaltine shake-up mug had been offered by Captain Midnight in the 1940s; and radio's Little Orphan Annie in the Depression years had kids drinking Ovaltine for pep and vigor. These shake-up mugs are among the collectibles that are sought out today by those who have a strong memory association with the Captain, the Orphan, and the Little Cowboy.

It was said that Howdy Doody resembled Charlie McCarthy's sidekick, Mortimer Snerd; and recently it was thought that he bore a striking similarity to a grinning peanut farmer named Jimmy Carter. (There is a collector's-item "Howdy Doody for President" button in which he is a Carter, or perhaps a JFK, lookalike.) Howdy Doody did symbolize the essence of the all-American 1950s kid dressed in cowboy gear, and many tired to emulate him in thought and deed. His cowboy-American philosophy, not unlike Hopalong Cassidy's (Hoppy always lectured the kids at sign-off

Howdy Doody cotton handkerchief.
Copyright Bob Smith.

time with a code-of-behavior message), was captured in a song the kids loved to sing:

> Never-ever-ever pick a fight,
> Cause it never-ever proves who's right.
>
> Be kind to animals,
> They think you're grand,
> Be kind to animals, they'll lick your hand.
> And take them for a regular walk
> And if they could talk, they'd say,
> Thanks for being kind to animals
> We love to be treated that way.
>
> My face may not be handsome
> I may be light or fair,
> But here in America,
> You're welcome, everybody's welcome . . .
>   everywhere.

Save your pennies, soon you'll have a nickel,
Save your nickels, soon you'll have a dime.

> Save your dimes, and soon you'll have a
>   quarter . . .
> And a quarter oughta make you awfully glad
>   you saved a dime.

Howdy Doody went off television on September 24, 1960, with an hour-long color retrospective. After sixteen years Howdy returned once again in 1976, as if to celebrate the Bicentennial. Program scheduling and too much format repetition are blamed for the failure of the 1970s Howdy revival; but even today Howdy Doody dolls and other items are still being produced to the delight of kids and their parents who refuse to forget. To many, "It's Howdy Doody time," the show's opening statement, still holds true for today. It seems Howdy Doody is an American legend, a pop culture icon for all time.

Howdy Doody "Chuck Wagon" lunch box,
Adco-Liberty, c. 1950. (P.C.)

Two Mickey Mouse cowboy stuffed cloth dolls with wooden shoes. Doll on right with movable arms is painted composition. Knickerbocker Toy Co., 1936. Copyright Walt Disney Enterprises. Ted Hake collection.

COWBOY MICKEY

The first sound cartoon, *Steamboat Willie,* opened at the Colony Theatre in New York on November 18, 1928, becoming an instant success for its creator, Walt Disney, and its hero, Mickey Mouse. Other cartoons followed. Mickey Mouse—the cheery imp rodent with a long tail, big black balloon ears, clown-size shoes, red shorts held up by two large buttons, two black ovals

with a wedge-shaped indentation for eyes, and a white face with a black stub of a nose—captivated a Depression-weary America. Disney created a merchandising empire with his sprightly mouse, and throughout the 1930s toys, Mickey Mouse soda pop, stuffed Mickey dolls, and hundreds of other items—today's collectibles— were everywhere: in the five-and-ten, in the grocery store, and in department stores and toy shops. Charlotte Clark and the

Knickerbocker Toy Company created some excellent stuffed dolls under Kay Kamen licensing; some of the most popular of these have Mickey dressed in cowboy attire.

Mickey went Western or South of the Border in several of his early cartoons, including *Gallopin' Gaucho* (1928), *The Cactus Kid* (1930), *Pioneer Days* (1930), and *Two Gun Mickey* (1934). In October 1935 he appeared on the cover of the *Mickey Mouse Magazine* in full cowboy gear, and a *Minnie Mouse–Mickey Mouse Doll Book* from the same period has Western cut-out clothes for Mickey and Minnie. Mickey may not have been real competition for Gene or Hopalong in cowboyland, but he certainly was a good-looking mouse dude.

"Mickey the Cowboy" ceramic planter, stamped on the bottom: "Mickey Mouse—Walt Disney Productions." c. 1940.

Throw rug of Mickey Mouse as a roping buckaroo, c. 1930. Created by Walt Disney and produced by Alexander Smith & Sons Carpet Co., Yonkers, New York.

Fast-draw cowboy electric mantel clock with revolving wire rope (missing), fake copper-bronze finish on white metal. United Manufacturers, c. 1940. Courtesy of Phases.

COWBOY STYLE

COWBOY DECO

Ranch-style Western decor is often an attempt to bring some of the outside elements of ranching indoors. The antique longhorn chair with intertwining horns covered in cowhide, mountain-lion skins, horsehair, or leopard velvet is a status symbol perfect for the Wild West den, as is the ladder-back chair with a cowhide seat. There might be a wagon-wheel light fixture hanging from the ceiling; a hickory table; a pine couch; an old relacquered trunk; a longhorn hat rack; and perhaps a display of white crockery. The room would also be a taxidermist's paradise, with mounted deer heads, a buffalo head, mounted fowl in flight, and a stuffed wildcat on the stone mantel. A prairie-cow's skull often is hung over the bar with the eyes lit from behind with a colored bulb. A patchwork quilt, a Mexican blanket, or an Indian rug would be hung on one wall, while on another would be an oil painting of cowboys rounding up cattle or a scene from the historic battle of the Alamo. A collector might also

have a display of Indian pottery, old barbed wire, or Winchester cartridge rifles and Remington guns. An old weathervane might be part of this authentic decor; and plants would be cactus if they were not made of plastic. Such would be the style of many a rancher's living room or den, or of an authentic Out-West hotel lobby, all of it accentuated by dark wood beams and paneling.

But the Old Texas or Western decor of this wagon-wheel variety is not of as much interest here as are the mass-produced decorations with a cowboy Western influence that came into the marketplace—the five-and-ten, the department store, and the hardware store—in the 1920s, '30s, '40s, and '50s. Average middle-brow Americans wanted to include some things with a Western motif in their homes without necessarily going all the way. This was particularly true in the 1940s and '50s, when ranch-style houses began to be constructed in the suburbs.

Western styles would sometimes be mixed with Mexicana in American household decor, particularly in the kitchen or den. You might, for instance, find a McCoy cowboy planter right next to a Mexican-wearing-a-sombrero-taking-a-siesta planter, which in turn would be alongside one of mother's countless Noritake ducks, rabbits, or dogs. There might be tumblers, tablecloths, or napkins with pictures of cowboys or cowgirls, or decal appliqués of one of the super-cowboys like Roy Rogers or Hopalong Cassidy might decorate the glass panel in a door. Salt shakers in the shape of boots and ceramic cowboy-hat ashtrays are examples of America's pop-culture style that has become so collectible today.

Cowboy wallpaper depicting ranch life would sometimes be used to cheer up a kitchen nook, but more often it was to be found in the den or, chiefly, in the boys' room along with bunk beds. These bunkhouse-style beds would often be of notched maple and had matching dressers and desks. There was also linoleum depicting cowboys and Indians for the boys' room. Part of the scheme would be a Roy Rogers or plain old cowboy lamp and a Gene

Autry toy chest. If a boy went Western, he usually wanted it "cowboy" all the way. In the 1940s draperies and bedspreads from Bates & Company were added, and if the fabric did not feature bombers or battleships in red, white, and blue, it depicted cowboys or Indians. Crockery or kitchenware had Western scenes with cowboy dudes, and there were cookie jars, plates, cups, glasses, and bowls featuring Hoppy, Gene, Roy, Bobby Benson, and the Lone Ranger.

A Monel metal mantel clock with a single cowboy in chaps sometimes was placed in the center of the mantel or on a bookshelf; and an ashtray in the shape of a horseshoe with a boot cigarette container would go along with it on the coffee table. Mass-produced items included spray-painted green metal cowboy statuette ashtrays, such as the one designed by John Held, Jr., in a comic style for Frankart, Inc. This type of item was sold at better gift shops or department stores; but a chalk or plaster amusement park statuette of the Lone Ranger, a cowgirl, or a buckaroo with

Decorative cowboy wallpaper borders. Top: *"Boots and Saddle."* Bottom: *"Arizona Cowboys." c. 1945. Dwight Goss Western-Collectibles collection.*

Ceramic cowboy planter produced by McCoy Pottery Company, c. 1940.

Souvenir Western boot cigarette container for the coffee table, bar, or desk; fake bronze-copper patina on white metal, c. 1940s. (P.C.)

Cowboy and cowgirl figurines. Hand-painted "Made in Japan" china knickknacks were sold in gift shops, five-and-tens, and department stores in the 1920s and 1930s. (P.C.)

Cowboy wallpaper from the 1940s in forest green. Courtesy Second Hand Rose.

his horse, spray-painted and pasted with glitter, could also be a colorful decor item when placed on top of the family console.

Framed pictures of cowboy heroes like Will Rogers, Gene Autry, and Tom Mix, bought at the five-and-ten or sent away for with cereal box tops, might hang right on the living-room wall. Father's Zane Grey books were held in place by ornate bronze bookends featuring cowboys, hats, boots, saddles, and the like. Reverse-painted glass shadow pictures of a lone cowboy on a hill-side, with a thermometer included and sometimes a calendar, hung in Dad's garage over the tool table. Cowboys were on the radio, in the movies, on television—why not at home?

Kitchen glass tumbler decorated with a cowboy on his horse, c. 1930s.

Vat-dyed cotton upholstery fabric, "Cowboy on Bull," slip-on snap pillow cover, c. 1939.

Woodgrain "Cowboy on the Range" wallpaper, 1940s. Courtesy Second Hand Rose.

Hopalong Cassidy "Bar 20" revolving-action mood lamp for the boys' room or den, 1949. Ted Hake collection.

Painted and pasted-with-glitter plaster amusement park cowgirl statue, c. 1930s. (P.C.)

Painted plaster "official" Roy Rogers desk lamp with the original paper shade, c. c. 1940s. Ted Hake collection.

Novelty comic cowboy ashtray, stamped "Frankart, Inc. 1928," designed by John Held, Jr., for Arthur Von Frankenberg. Depression-green paint on white metal.

COWBOY GEAR

The cowboy outfit of the early western frontier had to be economical and practical. A cowboy, like a farmer, was a worker; simplicity in dress was essential. A big wide-brimmed hat meant protection from the sun and other elements. Shirts in summer were cotton and in winter were wool. Dyes were very scarce, so often colors were blue, gray, brown, or black. Shirt pockets were nonexistent, and the poor stitching around the collar may have been one reason an early cowboy wore a bright bandanna, the other reason being to absorb sweat around the neck. The yoke front so popular in the design of Western shirts today originally provided added covering for the upper chest area in cold weather—and also helped blunt the effect of a cow's horns. Brighter colors, plaids, and checks came into fashion only after a time; silk shirts with embroidered Texas roses, snap closings, fringe, or fancy ribbing and piping around the yoke did not appear in frontier fashion until the time of the Wild West shows and the later rodeos. Some eccentric early cowgirls like Calamity Jane wore men's clothing, but usually women wore floor-length gingham-cotton dresses.

Today the standard clothing for a cowboy working a ranch would be a plaid or solid-color snap-button shirt that is tight at the wrists and tight-fitting blue jeans (never designer-label jeans or stretch jeans) worn with or without a belt. High boots with a pointed toe and sloped heel make it easier for the cowboy to get his foot into and out of the stirrup, and a big hat, usually a Stetson, tops off a work outfit that is designed for comfort on the job.

Fancy cowboy dress, the kind we associate with today's "urban cowboy," is sometimes

Metal-framed glass reverse-painted silhouette, cowboy and cowgirl pictures with "in-depth" background relief, c. 1930s.

What It Costs to Be a Well-Dressed Cowboy

By Scott Pierce

When a genuine cowboy star is all dressed up in his Sunday best, his glad rags represent a small fortune

Countless pages have been written about the cost of the feminine star's gowns, while the dyed-in-the-wool cowboy goes unsung

"Two-gallon" hat, $125

Shirt, $64; and 'kerchief, $35. Shirt of the heaviest possible satin, carefully stitched and tailored by hand. The silk 'kerchief is the size of a small table-cloth

Ornate gun-belt and holster, $375. Belt of finest quality leather, trimmed with white buckskin. Belt hand made, hand carved and hand stitched. Heavy buckle of solid silver and hand embossed

Belt, $35. Hand-carved throughout its length and with a solid silver buckle

Heavy calibre, pearl-handled six gun, $50

White buckskin chaps, $200. Of fine, pliable leather, surface studded with solid silver conchos

Ordinary work trousers, worn under the buckskin chaps, $15

High heel riding-boots, $45. Made of fine, pliable leather

Total cost of this outfit, worn by Jack Hoxie, is $1,269

Spurs of solid silver with gold inlay, fitted with white buckskin straps, $325. Hand made

A movie cowboy outfit that cost $1,269 in 1925 was the envy of all movie fans who yearned to dress "Hollywood-Wild-West" when they saw Jack Hoxie in this hand-on-hip macho pose in a film magazine of the day. Jim Hans collection.

RIDE 'EM COWBOY

Cowboy star, Roy Rogers, is wearing one
of his famous embroidered Western shirts.

GAY VARIETY OF "WESTERNS" FOR PLAYTIME

This young Roy Rogers' fan is jest rarin' to
rope 'em in his Yippee embroidered shirt.

Genial Roy Rogers, Republic Pictures'
popular cowboy star, who has sung his
way into the hearts of millions of fans in
his super-de-luxe Western films, has done
much to increase the popularity of the
gay Western shirt as a sportswear vogue.
Roy's life is busy—besides his radio program, and rodeo tours, he makes 8 pictures a year! Watch for "Apache Rose"
—Roy and Trigger are in color!

Western shirts, launched at smart Western resorts,
are now the active sports vogue. The gay embroidery
is in rodeo tradition. Mannish tailoring, bright colors
and close fit are the new characteristics of these shirts.

No. 1295, embroidered in satin stitch and chain. Sizes:
12-18. Size 16, 2½ yds. 35-in. Blue, yellow. 45c.

No. 1297, a razzle-dazzle version has attention-get-
ting contrast yoke, cuffs. Sizes: 12-18. Size 16, 2 yds.
35-in., ⅞ yd. 35-in. contrast. Yellow and blue. 45c.

No. 1310. Boys or girls will love a "Yippee" shirt!
Embroider shirt or appliqué it. Sizes: 6-12. Size 8, 1⅝
yds. 35-in., ⅝ yd. contrast. Blue, yellow transfer. 35c.

*Fashions of the 1940s with shoulder pads were inspired by the "flash cowboy"
outfits of Roy Rogers, from* McCall Needlework Magazine, *Summer 1947.*

so ornate that it is referred to as a Western costume—as in a theatrical wardrobe rental house. This type of outfit, which probably began with Buffalo Bill, is what we would look for today on a disco or country-music dance floor, or at a rodeo or dude ranch. The gaudier Western style was primarily developed by the Hollywood heroes, the "rhinestone cowboys." As well as being tapered and streamlined, this "flash cowboy" dress has a style that appeals to the vanity of the cowboy, city or country.

Broncho Billy Anderson liked to sport enormous sheepskin chaps on film, which were later avoided by Western stars who thought that only a city dude from the East would be caught wearing them. When he was horsing around, a slapstick sidekick

"Remington Derringer 1867" fancy novelty western-style belt buckle, chromium on white metal. There is a trick release for this miniature gun, which shoots caps. Manufactured by Mattel, 1959.

Advertisement for Texas Ranger Belts from 1947 Esquire magazine; the belts are similar to those found in western-style clothing shops today.

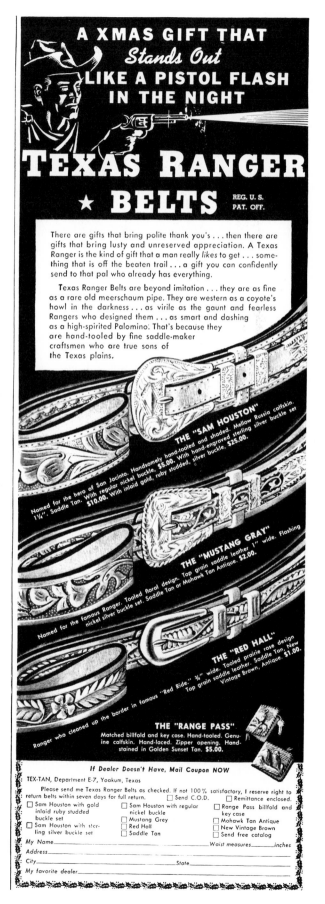

might put a pair on, but usually just for a laugh, which they always got.

Most early cinema cowboys, however, were less elaborate. William S. Hart maintained a penchant for the authentic in both his dress and manner. Hart's outfits were loose and casual; and he took pride in his cheap store-bought frontiersman-style shirts, plain frock coats, and dark baggy trousers.

Tom Mix was a showman whose costumes reflected the circus approach to Western apparel. He liked to wear elaborate outfits—finely sewn colored shirts, tight trousers with gold braid, and custom-made intricately carved boots. Mix introduced gloves, which were seldom worn by cowboys on the range.

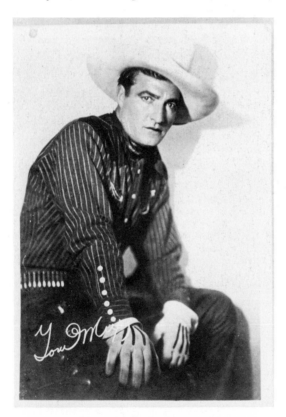

An early Tom Mix sendaway film studio publicity photo showing Tom in his typical fancy-dress cowboy shirt, neck scarf, gloves, and "Tom Mix" white hat. Ted Hake collection. (T.H.)

Gene Autry followed Tom Mix into the arena of the ostentatious movie cowboy getups, favoring jet-black shirts with white and gold braid. Both Autry and Mix liked to wear a big hat with a 7½″ crown and a 5″ brim. This hat eventually was produced for the market by Stetson and was called "The Tom Mix." In the 1940s Autry also wore bright cardinal-red shirts with Mexican flowers or a big American flag printed right across the front, almost as a pop-art emblem.

When Roy Rogers ascended over Gene Autry at Republic as "King of the Cowboys," his outfits went way beyond Autry's. Sequined, studded, or fringed shirts were as much a part of the Rogers image as his boyish grin and twinkling blue eyes. *Movie Life* of November 1948 contains an article entitled "The Rogers Look" in which Roy and Dale are shown in their favorite Western duds—matching suits of blue with inserts of darker blue, with maroon piping and arrows. The cowboy couple liked to wear matching Western suits with plenty of shoulder pads when they were showing themselves off at rodeos or in pictures, but at home they preferred colorful plaid shirts, bright neckerchiefs, blue jeans, cowboy hats, and handmade boots and belts; and that included all of the Rogerses' kids.

Initially Ken Maynard, Buck Jones, and Hoot Gibson enjoyed the streamlined look for cowboys and did not believe in overdressing for fear of looking like "drugstore cowboys." Gibson and Maynard finally went "flash" in the 1940s, but Buck Jones kept a distinctive simplicity. Big ten-gallon Stetson hats with pointy tops gave way in the 1940s, under Roy Rogers's influence, to a smaller version that had a wide brim but a smaller, indented crown.

Buckskin outfits with fringe were always popular and were favored by Johnny Mack Brown, Wild Bill Elliott, Gary Cooper, and Guy Madison. Good-guy cowboy movie heroes often wore all-white ensembles while the bad-guy villain wore all black. This concept worked particularly well in black-and-white "B" Westerns. William Boyd and Lash LaRue were exceptions to this rule, although Hoppy always rode a hero's white stallion. Tim McCoy and Gene Autry liked their black shirts with white piping topped off by a white hat.

Gun holsters and belts were ornate in Wild West Hollywood and were usually meticulously carved. Fancy accessories in Western wear include the bolo (string) tie, which usually has a ring with a cow's head or a horse on it. Collar tips, boot tips, and heel guards were often silver or gold. Belt buckles were usually the showiest item of a cowboy's outfit—also often silver or gold—with first or last names or names of states imprinted on them, as well as images of bucking broncos, bulls with long horns, or cowboys in action.

Silver Indian jewelry has been an aspect of Western culture since the frontier beginnings and has become one of today's most expensive collectibles (when it is authentic). Designs vary in sophistication according to the tribe, but the workmanship can be superb, mixing silver with turquoise and other semiprecious stones to produce dazzling rings, bracelets, buckles, slides, and other pieces.

Six Western horse-head dress or jacket pins in red, brown, and amber Catalin. They were mass-produced in the 1930s and 1940s.

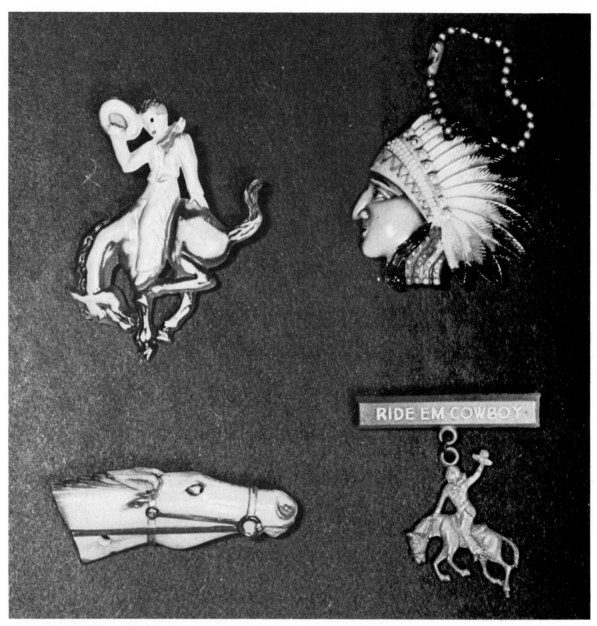

Bronco-buster cowboy pins, streamlined horse-head pin, and Indian-chief head key ring in celluloid, c. 1920.

On the more frivolous side of Western accessories is the Bakelite, celluloid (early plastic), or machine-carved wooden jewelry of the 1920s, '30s, and '40s, which would include buckaroos on their horses, hat and boot pins, horse heads, saddles, and lone cowboys, all purchased at rodeo souvenir stands, the five-and-ten, or a Western ranch gift shop. As decoration on a jacket or shirt, these mass-produced jewels—sometimes amusingly referred to as "Cobra Jewels" after Maria Montez in *Cobra Woman*—are very popular with nostalgia collectors today. (Everyone who saw Montez in her 1940s Technicolor movies knew her jewels were Hollywood-fake, but that only added to their make-believe value in the minds of viewers, and they did glitter as much as any that were real.)

Hand-carved leather or machine-tooled synthetic wallets from the 1930s, '40s, and '50s featuring Western themes, cowboys, howling prairie wolves, or boots are sought after by today's collectors—status symbols of yesterday's fashion recycled for today.

The popular "twin reindeer" all-wool sweaters of the 1940s from Jantzen and other companies featured bucking broncos, cowboys, mountain lions, wolves, steer heads, and buffalo, and these are being reproduced again by Stewart Richer for the Manhattan clothing firm Reminiscence. In 1980 an exact replica of the 1950s Hopalong Cassidy sweater flooded the market. Authentic sweaters can still be discovered, but they are rare and too often eaten up by moths. Children's Western-style outfits, particularly those featuring Roy, Hoppy,

Bakelite cowboy and horse jewelry from the five-and-dime, c. 1930. Courtesy A Touch of Us.

and Gene, may once again be back in the saddle when back-to-school fall fashions come around.

Ralph Lauren Western wear aside, it is important to note the growing number of antique clothing specialty shops in cities and towns across the country, in which the most highlighted and desirable items are Western. Gabardine cowboy shirts from the 1920s through the 1950s, with snap closings and sometimes embroidered flowers, cactus, hats, or bulls, are choice items among antique clothing collectors and enthusiasts. A shirt with long fringe will cost a bit more. If you are really a lucky buckaroo you may find one of these in a local thrift shop or Salvation Army store—but beware, the pros get there early in the morning. Flea market stalls and tables today also feature vintage clothing.

Leather pants, chaps, and vests are back in style, but these seldom show up in antique clothing bins, as any cowboy who owned a pair usually "just plain wore 'em out"—which would not be the case with a fancy shirt or a Tom Mix hat, usually kept as "special" and "treated right." In the 1880s fancy boots sometimes cost between $10 and $25. The sole of these boots was made of thin leather in order to get the feel of a stirrup. They also had to be worn skin tight to keep the foot "small" for the stirrup. The top of the boot was at least 17"

Embossed leather Gene Autry wallet, c. 1950.

"Saddle Craft" hand-tooled leather wallet by Textan of Yokum, Texas, featuring a "prairie wolf baying at the desert moon," c. 1930s. Courtesy Richard Utilla.

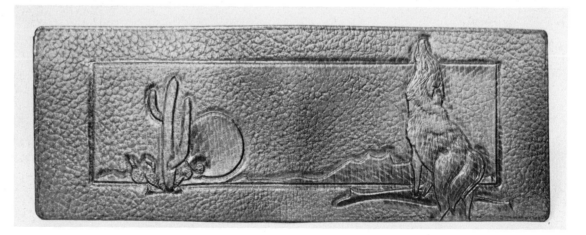

MILLER STOCKMAN

SUPPLY COMPANY **MILLER** WESTERN WEAR 1636-40 LAWRENCE ST.

DENVER COLORADO

LARGEST EXCLUSIVE DISTRIBUTOR
OF WESTERN WEAR IN
THE WORLD

PRICE CHANGES FOR CATALOG NO. 74

PAGE 14: BOOTS		
No. 664	Boots	11.50
No. 678	Boots	10.95
No. 683	Boots	10.95
No. 685	Boots	10.95
No. 688	Boots	11.95
No. 689	Boots	11.95

PAGE 15: BOOTS		
No. 625	Boots	$17.75
No. 626	Boots	17.75
No. 656	Boots	11.50
No. 657	Boots	12.95
No. 680	Boots	11.95
No. 681	Boots	11.95

PAGE 27: SHIRTS		
No. 135	Shirt	$ 6.50
No. 1201	Shirt	13.50

PAGE 49: BOOTS		
No. 614	Boots	$18.95
No. 615	Boots	18.95
No. 620	Shoes	15.50
No. 621	Shoes	15.50
No. 630	Shoes	16.50
No. 654	Boots	13.50

PAGE 50: BOOTS		
No. 602	Boots	$20.75
No. 617	Boots	22.95
No. 619	Boots	23.95
No. 655	Boots	11.75
No. 693	Boots	14.75

PAGE 51: BOOTS		
No. 622	Boots	$12.95
No. 623	Boots	12.95
No. 632	Boots	29.95
No. 633	Boots	23.50
No. 634	Boots	23.50
No. 638	Boots	24.75
No. 639	Boots	24.75
No. 671	Boots	19.50
No. 672	Boots	19.50
No. 675	Boots	12.95
No. 676	Boots	12.95
No. 682	Boots	19.50
No. 691	Boots	12.50
No. 692	Boots	12.50

CATALOG NO. 74 FALL & WINTER 1947-48

Miller Stockman of Denver, Catalogue #74, Fall and Winter, 1947–48. Cover.

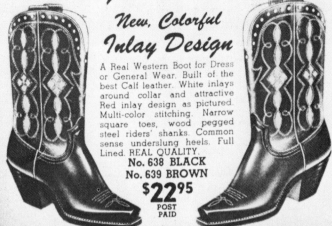

high so that pebbles or twigs could not get inside while riding. Heels were high, narrow, and sloped to hold into the stirrup, and a pointy toe helped a cowboy to slip in and out quickly. It was essential that boots help a rider slip free if thrown by a horse; a common accidental death for a cowboy was being dragged by a horse. Fine crafted boots in the old style are still being made by the better companies, which include Lucchese Boot Company of San Antonio, Justin Boot Company of Fort Worth, Tony

Hopalong Cassidy wrist guards in black leather with chrome metal studs. Ted Hake collection.

Hopalong Cassidy wallet, painted image on black cowhide, 1950.

184

COWBOY STYLE

Lama of El Paso, and Nocona Boot Company of Nocona; the original Frye boot (first designed in 1863 and still going strong today) and Acme Boots are preferred by working cowboys because of their combined toughness and low price.

The fancier hand carving and expensive materials like snakeskin, alligator, iguana

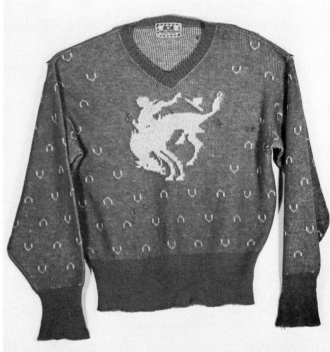

All-wool "Bucking Bronc Cowboy" sweater in red and white, CampusWear Sportswear, 1940s.

"Official" Hopalong Cassidy all-wool black and white sweater (with Topper on the reverse side), Barklay Knitwear, 1950s.

Wool "Roy Rogers" Western outerwear sports jacket in light tan with dark-brown trim. Irving Foster, c. 1950. Courtesy Richard Utilla.

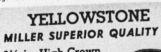

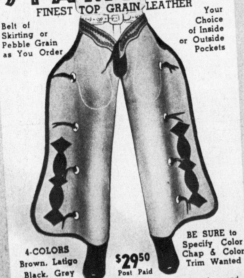

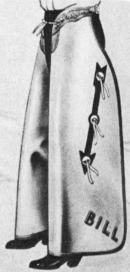
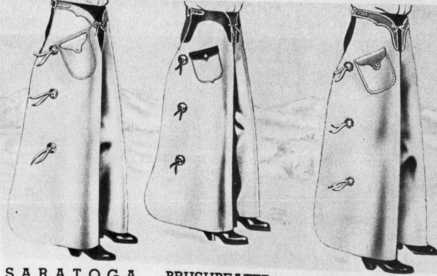
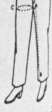

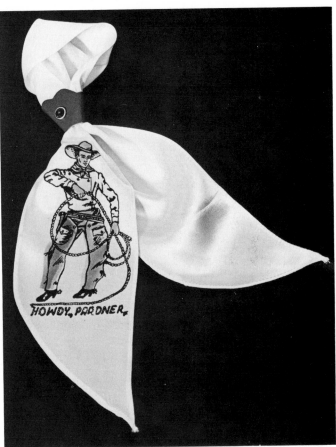

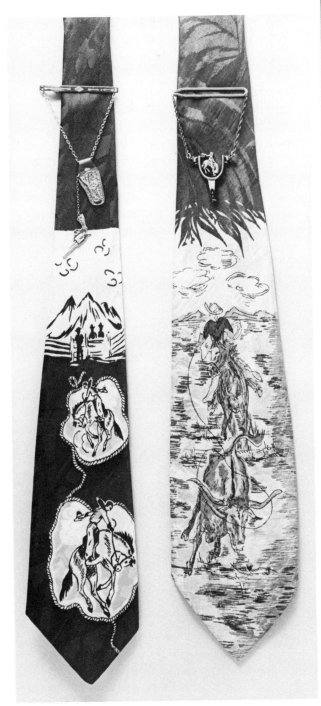

lizard, or buffalo hide bring the price up. Cowhide is still the most practical material and the least costly, and spurs still can be attached if you must kick up the dust. Boots and other items with an authentic western "feel" can be found at many specialty shops such as H. Kauffman & Sons Saddlery in New York. Naturally, Texas

Above: Satin cowboy "Windsor" neckerchief with handpainted buckaroo and leather scarf holder with jeweled stud, late 1930s. Silk-screen gentleman's tie (far left) and hand-painted silk tie (near left) from Speakeasy Antiques. Tie clasps courtesy Peanut Butter and Jane. All from the 1940s.

and the other Western states are filled with this type of store, including Cutter Bill Western World, in Dallas, and the world's largest Western store chain, Shepler's, headquartered in Wichita, Kansas.

In addition to collecting antique clothing and jewelry with a Western flavor, many cowboy buffs like to collect old catalogues of Western wear (with original prices). Surprisingly little has changed in cowboy styles since the 1920s and even earlier. As you glance through these catalogues from Sears, Roebuck or H. Kauffman or Miller Stockman, you will note the simplicity of the Western styles, which are not dated and have become, as many folks today like to say, "back in the saddle" classics.

Dressing up "cowboy" is not only a practical manner of dress; it can also be fashion fun. That urban or dude cowboy swaggering down the city street may never have roped a cow, pulled down a steer, or jumped on a bronc, but it doesn't mean he isn't macho as long as he feels that way. Kids play at cowboy; and adults now seem to enjoy it too.

Cowboy outfits for boys from Butler Brothers catalogue, Christmas, 1934.

*A young buckaroo in a Butler
Brothers cowboy outfit, 1934.*

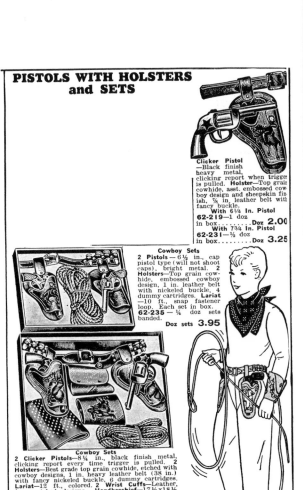

*Pistol and holster sets for boys,
Butler Brothers Catalogue, 1934.*

COWBOY AND INDIAN COMIC VALENTINES

The confrontation of cowboys and Indians entered the dimestore world of most American kids throughout the year, but Valentine's Day was always a special day to send cowboy, cowgirl or Indian messages of love to a classmate or special pal.

The comic graphics on many of the early 1920s, '30s, or '40s valentines, which often cost no more than a single copper penny, were colorful and cheerful and a great way to send heartfelt love. If a kid had a crush on another kid, what better way was there to express these feelings than with a "Howdy, Pardner!," a slap on the back, and a comic valentine, western style, on February 14. After all, Cowboys and Indians was the favorite game of America's kids.

Cowboy valentine from the five-and-dime, c. 1930.

Accordion foldout valentine with comic "Injuns" was sent to a classmate in Depression-era America.

If you pull the top of Charlie McCarthy's cowboy hat, his eyes will move and his mouth will shut, just as any good ventriloquist's dummy should. A paper comic "Made in U.S.A." Valentine's Day card, c. 1938.

TRAIL'S END: HAPPY HAMBURGER TO YOU!

Vast stretches of land of natural beauty continue to remain a part of the great American Western terrain, but today these areas are also referred to by environmentalists as "a vanishing wilderness" in need of watchful governmental protection lest they disappear altogether under the encroachment of industry, toxic waste, urbanization, and other effects of the technological age.

Travel by jet and superhighway has narrowed the gap between city and country. With fast-speed turnpikes has come a new and monotonous standardization symbolized by fast food hamburger chains like Roy Rogers, Arby's, and McDonald's,

Arby's Drive-in Restaurant highway road sign at night outside the Holland Tunnel entrance to New York City in Jersey City, New Jersey.

which dot the landscape in cities, along highways, and in shopping centers. Often these hamburger "joints" have a Western motif incorporated into their decor and serve hamburgers or Western barbecue-style roast beef sandwiches in specially designed wrappings or cardboard boxes. Some of these boxes, paper cups, and other modern packaging items from Roy Rogers, Arby's, or the other restaurants may well be on their way to becoming the new cowboy collectibles for tomorrow. Beef has always been the business of cowboys, so it seems appropriate at "trail's end" to close with the image of a packaged-fast-food hamburger created for consumption for the entire family—mom, pop, and the kids.

The first of the Western-style chain of restaurants serving steak and other good food at affordable prices were opened as depot eateries along the Santa Fe Railroad line as far back as the late 1870s by Frederick Henry Harvey. Harvey had the novel idea of bringing in attractive women, many of them from the East, to work in his restaurants. Five thousand of the Harvey Girls, as they came to be known, eventually settled down in the sparsely populated Old West as wives of ranchers, farmers, and cowboys.

In the 1920s and '30s, with the advent of modernism as a new way of life, many quick-cook hamburger chains were built along newly paved highways and in growing towns and cities across America. The first of these was the White Castle System

McDonald's hamburger chain giveaway "Buck Barry" iron-on transfer is a current cowboy collectible, c. 1980.

Right: *Roadside sign. Roy Rogers Family Restaurants serve fast-food hamburgers and french fries. This one, on Route 24 in Millburn, New Jersey, is decorated with original Roy Rogers movie posters and lobby cards.*

Roy Rogers "instant" cowboy collectibles, c. 1980. Soft-drink paper cups, Roy Rogers Bar-B-Q Sauce in a plastic container, and RR Burger wrappers. Picture of Roy Rogers, "King of the Cowboys," with Trigger is an "in color" Republic Studios sendaway from the 1940s.

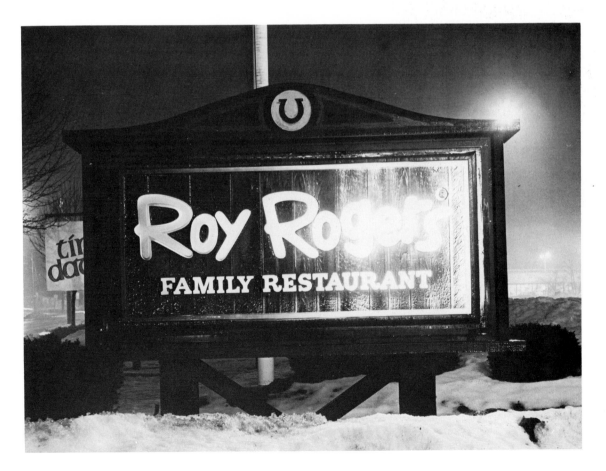

("Buy 'em by the sack"), which originally opened in 1921 selling tiny square-shaped 5-cent hamburgers prepared in stainless-steel-and-enameled kitchens. Millions were served to satisfied customers, along with a cup of steaming hot coffee and a cruller. White Castles are still offering Americans these small-sized ground-beef hamburgers in "sanitary" blue and white miniature "castle" boxes, but other hamburger chains from the era of early modernism seem to be on the wane, if they haven't gone out of business altogether—the Red Beacon, the Blue Castle, the White Diamond, and the White Tower, to name just a few. The bright-orange Stewart's stands continue serving hot dogs and hamburgers along with root beer in a frosted glass mug on car trays in 1930s roadside style. The Howard Johnson's chain, though not as attractive as it used to be, now serves hamburger patties and other bland ready-made food along with its many flavors of ice cream.

Whether a cowboy of the Old West, if he were able to be transported out of the past into the mass-produced hamburger world of today, would enjoy a soft, gummy packaged hamburger as much as he would have enjoyed a sizzling Harvey Girls steak must remain among the unanswerables. Trail-blazing cowboys liked "good workingmen's grub," so if this old-time Westerner could not easily find a ready steak hereabout at a decent price, he might be satisfied by a bowl of Tex-Mex red chili, which is having a revival throughout the country.

As we began with the open land, cowboys, and cattle, it seems appropriate to end with the landscape and beef, albeit hamburger. Eating a barbecue-burger or one of the other varieties of hamburger at a Roy Rogers city or highway restaurant, one can relax and enjoy, contemplating the days of the Old West movieland style, while looking at the photo blow-ups of Roy, Dale, and Trigger that usually adorn the walls. The dream of riding the Western range on a horse and singing a "happy trail" cowboy song will never die—at least not in the imagination—whether the influence is real, legendary, or Hollywood.

Gigantic two-gun painted metal cowboy road sign lights up in neon at night. Neon moving hand signals highway night riders and truckers to "drive in" for "true Western hospitality in a pioneer atmosphere." The New Village Family Restaurant is on Route 9, Atlantic City Boulevard, Bayville, New Jersey. The proprietor is Louis "Tex" Gotsis.

BIBLIOGRAPHY

Beadle's Dime Library (facsimile of 1882 edition). Austin, Texas: Steck-Vaughn, 1965.

Butel, Jane. *Chili Madness*. New York: Workman, 1981.

Carter, Randolph. *The World of Flo Ziegfeld*. New York: Praeger, 1974.

Dary, David. *Cowboy Culture*. New York: Knopf, 1981.

DeLano, Sharon, and Rieff, David. *Texas Boots*. New York: Viking, 1981.

D. L. Starbuck's and D. L. Jardine's Texas Foods. Austin, Tex.: 1981 (recipe pamphlet).

Dobie, J. Frank. *Cow People*. Boston: Little, Brown, 1964.

———. *Prefaces*. Boston: Little, Brown, 1975.

Everson, William K. *A Pictorial History of the Western Film*. Secaucus, N.J.: Citadel Press, 1969.

Eyles, Allen. *The Western*. New York: A. S. Barnes, 1975.

Felbinger, Lee J. *The Lone Ranger Pictorial Scrapbook*. Green Lane, Pa.: Countryside Advertising, 1979.

Fenin, George N., and Everson, William K. *The Western*. New York: Penguin, 1977.

Forbis, William H. *The Old West: The Cowboys*. New York: Time-Life Books, 1973.

Goodstone, Tony, ed. *The Pulps*. New York: Chelsea House, 1970.

Griffith, Richard. *The Talkies*. New York: Dover, 1971.

Grossman, Gary H. *Saturday Morning TV*. New York: Dell, 1981.

Hake, Theodore L., and Cauler, Robert D. *Six Gun Heroes*. Des Moines: Wallace-Homestead, 1976.

Hassrick, Royal B. *The Colorful Story of the American West*. Rev. ed. New York: Crown, 1978.

Hine, Robert V. *The American West*. Boston: Little, Brown, 1973.

Horan, James D. *The Great American West*. Rev. ed. New York: Crown, 1978.

———. *The Lawmen*. New York: Crown, 1980.

Horwitz, James. *They Went Thataway*. New York: Dutton, 1976.

Jim Harmon's Nostalgia Catalogue. Los Angeles: Tarcher, 1973.

Kauffman, Sandra. *The Cowboy Catalog*. New York: Clarkson Potter, 1980.

Kent, Rosemary. *The Genuine Texas Handbook*. New York: Workman, 1981.

Ketchum, William C., Jr. *Western Memorabilia*. Maplewood, N.J.: Hammond, 1980.

Lesser, Robert. *A Celebration of Comic Art and Memorabilia.* New York: Hawthorn, 1975.

McDowell, Bart. *The American Cowboy in Life and Legend.* Washington, D.C.: National Geographic, 1972.

Merk, Frederick. *History of the Westward Movement.* New York: Knopf, 1978.

Neely, Martina, and Neely, William. *The International Chili Society Official Chili Cookbook.* New York: St. Martin's Press, 1981.

Nicholas, John H. *Tom Mix Riding up to Glory.* Oklahoma City: Persimmon Hill Publication, National Cowboy Hall of Fame and Western Heritage Center, 1980.

1981 Official Pro Rodeo Media Guide. Colorado Springs: Professional Rodeo Cowboys Association, 1981.

O'Brien, P. J. *Will Rogers.* Philadelphia: John C. Winston, 1935.

O'Neil, Paul. *The Old West: The End and the Myth.* Alexandria, Va.: Time-Life Books, 1979.

Overstreet, Robert M. *The Comic Book Price Guide.* New York: Harmony Books, 1970.

Penfield, Thomas. *Western Sheriffs and Marshals.* New York: Grosset & Dunlap, 1955.

Rothel, David. *The Singing Cowboys.* S. Brunswick, N.J.: A. S. Barnes, 1978.

Savage, William W., Jr. *The Cowboy Hero.* Norman: University of Oklahoma Press, 1979.

Seiverling, Richard F. *Tom Mix & Tony.* Hershey, Pa.: Keystone Enterprises, 1980.

Sell, Henry Blackman, and Weybright, Victor. *Buffalo Bill and the Wild West.* New York: Oxford, 1955.

Tanner, Ogden. *The Old West: The Ranchers.* Alexandria, Va.: Time-Life Books, 1977.

Tolbert, Frank X. *A Bowl of Red.* Garden City, N.Y.: Doubleday, 1966.

INDEX

(Page numbers in italics refer to illustrations.)

Ovaltine shake-up mugs, 159

Pacific Playing Card Company, 135
Painted Desert, The (film), 122, 145
Painted Ponies (film), 36
Pals of the Golden West (film), 111
Pancho, *see* Cisco Kid and Pancho
Paperbacks, Western, 23–25, 28–29, *29*
Paper collectibles, 28–29
Paramount Pictures, 66, 111
Parker, Bonnie, 68
Parker, Fess, 141
Partners of the Plains (film), 125–126
Paul, Les, 98
Payne, John, 140
Peck, Gregory, 148
Pecos Bill, 23, 118
Pendleton Round-up Official Souvenir Program, *xii*
Penny Books, 27
Perils of Nyoka (film), 70
Peter the Great (dog), 39
Phantom Empire (film), 95
Plainsman, The (film), 145
Polyscope Movie Company, 44, 46
Popular Melodies (publisher), 131
Porter, Cole, 111
Porter, Edwin S., 33
Post, Wiley, 42
Postcards, collecting, 28
Post Cereals, 115, 138
Powell, Dick, 62
Powell, Lee, 70
Powell, Teddy, 91–92
Prairie Thunder (film), 143
Public Cowboy No. 1 (film), 96
Pulps, *15*, 28
dime novels and, 23–25
Purvis, Melvin, 68

Quaker Oats, 112, 115
Quick magazine, *96*

Radio shows
Gene Autry's, 95, 97–98
Bobby Benson's Adventures, 62, 87–88
Hopalong Cassidy's, 127–128
Cisco Kid's, 89
Death Valley Days, 88–89, 147
Lone Ranger's, 64–67, 70, 74
Tom Mix's, 50–53, 62
popularity of (1930s), 62–63
Red Ryder's, 84
Roy Rogers's, 112, 115
Railroads
granting of land to, 20
transcontinental, 20
western expansion of, 15, 17
Rainbow over Texas (film), 111
Ralston, Vera Hruba, 110
Ralston Purina Company, 49, 50, 51, 52
Ranch Life in the Great South West (film), 44
Rancho Notorious (film), 146

Randall, Jack, 143
Range Feud (film), 145
Range Rider, The (TV show), 98
Rawhide, 3–4
RCA Victor, 118
Reagan, Nancy (Davis), 115, 147
Reagan, Ronald, 115, *146*, 146–147
films, 147
Red Raiders (film), 36
Red River (film), 145
Red River Range (film), 145
Red River Valley (film), 96, 111
Red Ryder, 27, 84–85
books, 84, *84*, 85–87
collectibles, *85*, 85–87, *86*
comics, 85
films, 85
Red Ryder (radio show), 84
Regular Scout, A (film), 36
Reid, Wallace, 122
Renegade Ranger, The (film), 145
Republic Pictures, 64, 70, 95–96, 110, 113, 118
Republic Studios, 105, 106, 140
Restaurants, fast-food, *191–194*, 191–195
Return of Jesse James, The (film), 146
"Rhinestone cowboys," 175
Rhythm on the Range (film), 106
sheet music from, *154*
Ride 'Em Cowboy (film), 145
Ride, Ranger, Ride (film), 96
Riders of the Purple Sage, 112
Ringling Brothers Circus, 36
Rin Tin Tin, 37, 39, *39*
Ritter, Tex, 88, 143, 145
comics, *142*, 155
River of No Return, The (film), 145
RKO, 122
Road to Yesterday (film), 122
Robbins, Music, 118
Roberts, Oral, 115
Rocky Mountaineers (group), 105–106
Rodeos, 31
origin of, 1–2
Rodgers, Jimmie, 91
Rodgers, Richard, 148, 150
Rogers, Cheryl, 105
Rogers, Ginger, 62, 148
Rogers, Linda Lou, 105
Rogers, Roy, 27, 29, 36, 72, 96, 147
books, *112*, 116–117
characterized, 112
collectibles, *104, 107–115*, 115–118, *116, 117, 119, 166, 171, 184, 193*
comics, 116
cut-out dolls, *111*, 117
early life and show-business career of, 105–108
fast-food restaurants of, 191–192, *193*, 195
films, 106, 108–111
museum (Victorville, California), 115
music, *108*, 112, 114, 117–118
outfits worn by, *174*, 176
postcard, *xiv*

Rogers, Roy *(cont.)*
radio show, 112, 115
religiousness of, 114–115
television series, 112–114, 115, 129
watches and clocks, 118, *119*
Rogers, Roy, Jr. ("Dusty"), 105
Rogers, Will, 41–42, *42, 43*, 44, 169
and Gene Autry, 94, 95, 96
death of, 42–43, 49
funeral souvenir program for, *42*
Romance on the Range (film), 111
Rooney, Mickey, 97, 148, *153*
Roosevelt, Teddy "Cowboy," 41, 42–43
Rooster Cogburn and the Lady (film), 145
Rose-Marie (film), 150
Roundup, 2, 5–6, 11
Roundup Time in Texas (film), 96
Rubbertone, 138
Russell, Jane, 111, 148
Rustlers' Valley (film), 126
Ryder, Red, *see* Red Ryder

Saalfield Publishing, 27, 57, 89
Sagebrush Trail (film), 145
Sagebrush Troubador (film), 96
St. John, Al "Fuzzy," 141
Saloons, 15–16
Salute (film), 143
Sam B. Dill Circus, 49
Samuel Lowe Company, 124, 129–130
Samuels, Walter, 91
Sands of Iwo Jima (film), 145
Santa Anna, Antonio López, 3
Santa Fe Trail, The (film), 147
Scott, Fred, 143
Scott, Randolph, 146
Scourge of the Desert, The (film), 35
Sears, Roebuck Company, 95, 188
Sebastian, Dorothy, 122
Second Hand Rose, 168, 170
Selander, Lesley, 126
Selig, William, 44, 46
Sells-Floto Circus, 48
Selznick, David O., 140
Señor Daredevil (film), 36
Serbaroli, Hector E., *He Lit the Genial Fires of Friendship*, 43
Shawnee Trail, 4
Sheridan, Ann, 147
Sheriff of Tombstone (film), 111
Sherman, Harry "Pop," 121, 122–123, 125
Sherman, Teddi, *149*
She Wore a Yellow Ribbon (film), 145
Short, Luke, 28
Shutta, Ethel, 148
Siegel, Sol, 106
Sielke, L., Jr., 35
Siesta (Lon Megargee), *10*
Silver (Lone Ranger's horse), 64, 66, 70, 72
collectibles, 77, 80, 83
comic book, *66*, 77
Silvercup Bread, 67, 74, 78
Silverheels, Jay, 71, *75*

About the Authors

As a collector of popular culture, Robert Heide has published feature articles in the *Village Voice,* the *Soho Weekly News, Portfolio, Antiques World,* and other publications; he has lectured on the subject at the Smithsonian Institution (Cooper Hewitt), the Delaware Art Museum, and the Park Avenue Armory "Winter Antiques" Show. Mr. Heide is also well known as a playwright for such productions as *The Bed, Moon, At War with the Mongols,* and *Suburban Tremens.*

John Gilman has created popular-culture exhibitions in conjunction with the New York Art Deco Exposition at Radio City Music Hall, the National Antiques Show at Madison Square Garden, and the Queens Museum Exhibition of the 1939–1940 World's Fair; he has lectured at the Smithsonian Institution and the Delaware Art Museum and has published articles in *Infinity, Portfolio,* and the *Village Voice.* Mr. Gilman has also served as the executive director of the American Society of Magazine Photographers.

The authors have also written *Dime-Store Dream Parade: Popular Culture 1925–1955.*